The Vampire of

Sacramento

The True Story of Richard Chase
The Blood-Thirsty Cannibal

True Crime Explicit Volume 1

Genoveva Ortiz, True Crime Seven

TRUE CRIME Z

ISBN: 9798658801346

Table of Contents

Explore the Stories of

The Murderous Mind

A Note

From True Crime Seven

Hi there!

Thank you so much for picking up our book! Before you continue your exploration into the dark world of killers, we wanted to take a quick moment to explain the purpose of our books.

Our goal is to simply explore and tell the stories of various killers in the world: from unknown murderers to infamous serial killers. Our books are designed to be short and inclusive; we want to tell a good scary true story that anyone can enjoy regardless of their reading level.

That is why you won't see too many fancy words or complicated sentence structures in our books. Also, to prevent the typical cut and dry style of true crime books, we try to keep the narrative easy to follow while incorporating fiction style storytelling. As to information, we often find ourselves with too little or too much. So, in terms of research material and content, we always try to include what further helps the story of the killer.

Lastly, we want to acknowledge that, much like history, true crime is a subject that can often be interpreted differently. Depending on the topic and your upbringing, you might agree or disagree with how we present a story. We understand disagreements are inevitable. That is why we added this note, so hopefully, it can help you better understand our position and goal.

Now without further ado, let the exploration to the dark begin!

Introduction

HUMANS ARE FASCINATED BY EVIL. POP culture is full of mad men, killers, and monsters who have become iconic characters, and sometimes are even more beloved than the heroes.

Villains make a story interesting, and no matter how depraved they may be, there is always a part of us that almost wants to see them win. After all, the higher the stakes, the more powerful the story.

When we get older, however, we learn that true evil really does exist. A real-life villain does not need to be a criminal mastermind or a mad scientist. Sometimes, evil is merely a human being hiding in plain sight.

Human monsters can turn our world upside down. Suddenly, the neighborhoods we have called home all our lives become dangerous, and the people we call our friends become suspects. When a killer strikes, can the people around the victims ever feel safe again?

Richard Chase changed the lives of multiple people in the most nightmarish ways imaginable. It was not enough for him to simply take the lives of his victims; he also drank their blood and violated their bodies for his own twisted curiosity. He killed without remorse, and scariest of all, he killed without rhyme or reason. Anyone was fair game to the *Vampire of Sacramento*.

But at the end of the day, Richard Chase was still only human, and his story is not only one of horror and disgust, but also a tragedy about an extremely sick person who was failed by his family and mental health professionals alike. Had someone taken Chase's alarming behavior seriously when he was young, would six innocent people still be alive?

Was Chase destined to become a killer, or did life mold him into one?

This book will explore not only the terrible crimes perpetrated by one of the world's most horrific and depraved murderers, but also examine the social conditions that allowed him to become a monster.

I

A Troubled Boy

LONG BEFORE HE EVER DRANK THE BLOOD OF people and animals, Richard Trenton Chase lived an unassuming life. Born on May 23rd, 1950, in Santa Clara County, California, to Richard Chase Sr., a computer specialist, and Beatrice, a teacher, Richard appeared in his earliest years to be an average boy—nothing special, though nothing peculiar, either.

When he was three years old, his family managed to afford to move into a house in Sacramento, and the next year, his sister Pamela was born. He was a Cub Scout and played four years of little league baseball. Young Richard was well-liked by his teachers, who all thought he was a sweet child, and he was popular with his peers, with dozens of them coming to attend his birthday parties.

On the surface, the Chases were just like any other family building a life for themselves in mid-century America. However, things at home were a different story.

The 1950s were a polarizing time in American history. Many fondly recall the era's economic prosperity and the growing middle class. It was the age of rock 'n' roll and televisions, but it was also the time when the nuclear family values reigned supreme. Husbands and fathers were the heads of the house, and the rest of the family obeyed. It is little surprise then that, at the time, Richard Chase's childhood was considered to have been unmarred by abuse, especially so when compared to the early lives of other serial killers.

Richard's parents were strict disciplinarians who doled out punishment regularly. When he was only two years old, he was force-fed by his father until he vomited. Pamela Chase would later recall confrontations between her brother and their father that ended with Richard Sr. shaking the boy or throwing him against the wall. The elder Richard was allegedly also emotionally abusive and yelled at his son whenever the boy messed something up.

Due to the elder Richard's difficulty managing money and alcoholism, the parents also had marital problems and often fought, usually loudly, in front of their young children. Beatrice Chase, on the other hand, had the tendency to accuse her husband of "using dope" and trying to poison her. As the years went on, she also began accusing Richard Sr. of infidelity with their neighbors, once even claiming that he was cheating while the family was on a camping trip in Oregon.

Preoccupied with their crumbling marriage, Richard's parents paid little attention to their quiet son and the strange behaviors he began to exhibit. When he was ten years old, Richard developed a grim interest with dead animals. He liked to kill and torture cats that he found around the neighborhood. He was fascinated by their blood and insides in a way that seemed almost clinical.

It started with cats, but Richard would later begin killing birds, rabbits, and dogs. At one point, the young boy had killed so many stray cats that neighbors took notice of their sudden disappearances. Among her flowers, Beatrice found one buried in the soil.

Life got worse at home over the next few years. When he was 12, his parents' fighting reached a boiling point, and his mother saw two different psychiatrists for emotional issues. At 13, his parents went through economic hardship and lost their house. All the while, Richard was still exhibiting troubling behaviors.

When he was around 13, Richard experienced one of his earliest breaks from reality. He became convinced that he was actually a member of the James-Younger Gang, a group of outlaws from the 19th century that included the notorious Jesse James. He got a poster made of the gang that had his picture pasted onto it and repeatedly asked his mother to buy him a cowboy hat.

Richard also developed the strange habit of burning pans while trying to cook for himself in the middle of the night. He tended to leave puddles on the kitchen floor and made messes that he made no effort to clean up. At other times, he would turn the heat up in the house to over 90 degrees whenever he was alone, strip off his clothing, and spend the night lying on the couch in the living room. He liked to play with matches and would often set small fires.

He still wet the bed.

The Macdonald Triad, also known as the Triad of Sociopathy, is a set of behaviors thought to be predictive of violent behavior when observed in childhood. The three behaviors are: animal cruelty, frequent bed-wetting past the age of five, and arson. Richard exhibited all three.

By the time Richard was in high school, his parents had had enough of each other. They separated, and Beatrice took her children to Los Angeles to live with relatives when Richard was in the middle of ninth grade. Only eight days later, Richard Sr. followed, intent on bringing his son back to Sacramento. Four months later, Beatrice and Pamela came back home.

Back at school, Richard, known as Rick to his classmates, seemed to have no trouble fitting in. He kept himself well-groomed and was decently popular, even going on a few dates with girls.

There were two girls in particular whom he dated seriously, and one relationship he had with a girl named Libby Christopher lasted for an entire year. However, both of these relationships would come to an end for the same embarrassing reason. He was attracted to women, but when it came down to actually having sex, he could not express his attraction. The girls he dated broke up with him once they realized he could not maintain an erection.

Richard was humiliated. Chronically underweight and impotent, he began to feel weak and broken. His defective penis became a point of obsession for him throughout his life and perhaps sparked one of his earliest and most constant delusions.

In Richard's mind, his erectile dysfunction was the cause of a lack of blood. To fix this, he needed to consume the blood of animals.

II

The Madness Begins

STILL POPULAR ENOUGH TO BE INVITED TO parties, Richard began to drink quite often. At one party, he ended up drinking too much and behaved erratically, running down the street screaming and making noises that no one could understand. One of his friends became concerned and took him home. Alone together, Richard finally confided in the other boy about his impotence. It was taking a toll on him, affecting him deeper than he let on.

Certainly not making matters any easier was Richard's drug use. Like any rebellious teenager in the 1960s, he had begun to experiment with marijuana, though he also took large amounts of

LSD and amphetamines. Gone was the sweet, considerate Cub Scout who passed his time playing baseball. In his place now was a moody teenager who hung out with acidheads and showed no remorse for stealing from neighbors or hurting animals.

The elder Richard was disappointed in his son. The boy had no sense of direction, had no discipline or values. It got worse when he was 15 and had his first run-in with the law for possession of marijuana in 1965. Though Richard denied taking drugs, the juvenile court ordered the boy to do community clean-up work on the weekends, a punishment his father did not protest.

The fact that Richard Sr. did not hire a lawyer to defend him made his son upset, adding to his growing resentment of his family.

His grades began to slip, going from Cs and Ds to Fs. Richard no longer cared about school. As far as anyone could tell, he had no ambition. Little else mattered aside from drugs and blood. Still, he managed to graduate from Mira Loma High School in June of 1968, and his parents bought him a Volkswagen as a present.

In 1969, at the age of 18, Richard was still suffering from that same embarrassing problem. His erectile dysfunction distressed him so much that he sought help from a psychiatrist. Not only was he seeking help for his impotence, but his own emotional instability was worrying him, and his parents' constant fighting and financial troubles added to his stress.

Richard was told that his erectile dysfunction was caused by an emotional issue, likely anxiety or repressed rage toward women. The psychiatrist suspected that his patient was mentally ill, but not so much so that he needed intervention. Ultimately, this was of little help to Richard, who still believed that his body was low on blood.

As time went on, he suffered quietly. He grew his hair long and began to neglect his hygiene, giving him a constantly disheveled appearance. He lived in filth and began to withdraw more and more from other people. His friends stopped coming by the house.

Though his father was worried, Beatrice thought nothing of her son's slovenly looks. It was the 60s, after all—the age of hippies and debauchery. The grimy, unkempt look was in, and therefore, Richard was like any other teenager at the time. She refused to consider the possibility that her son's appearance was the result of any real problem.

In late 1968, he finally got a job as a typist that he held for some time with the Retailers Credit Association. According to his mother, his work was more than satisfactory. He also began to think about going to college, a decision his parents encouraged. Eventually, he enrolled at American River College.

Despite his inner turmoil, his parents were hopeful that their son was getting his life together.

But this hope would not last long.

III

The Weirdo

RICHARD CHASE SAT OUTSIDE ON THE STOOP of a house, huffing to himself.

He didn't have anywhere to live now that the school no longer wanted him. He had done poorly in college, lacking focus, and never deciding on a career path. His grades were low, and all the enthusiasm he'd had for continuing his education was gone. For a time, he stopped going to classes for what he called a "leave of absence." However, American River College did not approve of this action, and he was expelled.

Two young women saw him sitting on the stoop, and one of them recognized him. They had gone to high school together, and the woman, still thinking of Richard as the well-mannered, handsome boy she had known, struck up a conversation with him. The three of them talked. It was good to see Rick Chase again, even if he had stopped brushing his hair.

Richard opened up about his situation, and the women were sympathetic. The house he was sitting outside of turned out to belong to them—and they had space for a third roommate. They invited Richard to move in with them, an offer he quickly accepted. He got a room and space of his own. Best of all, his parents, who provided him with rent money, did not have to know about his latest failure.

He moved in, and in no time, he would overwhelm his new roommates.

His drug habit had not gotten any better. While marijuana was still his drug of choice, he was also using LSD. He was constantly high, making it difficult for his roommates to reason with him when his behavior became particularly baffling.

Paranoia preoccupied his mind. He believed that somebody was after him, and he needed to get away in order to keep people from sneaking up on him. He boarded his bedroom door closed, knocked a hole in his closet wall, and then nailed shut the closet door from the inside.

Unable to hold down a stable job, Richard was up making noise at all hours. His roommates quickly grew tired of him, but the worst was yet to come.

He was a filthy person. He seldom bathed and never did his own laundry. This gave him a very noticeable, foul smell that the roommates found repulsive. Once, when one of the women had some female friends over, the rank-smelling Richard emerged naked from his bedroom and sat on the couch with the women. He tried to start a conversation, but his words were all incoherent.

When the women threw a party, they worried about what their strange roommate might do. Things seemed fine at first, but as the night went on, Richard began to act up again. He got down on the floor of the living room in the middle of the party and started moaning and making other unintelligible noises.

At another party, Richard's paranoia took over, and he spent the night leaning out the window, waving a gun at passing strangers. Rick Chase terrified his roommates, and they knew they needed him out of the house.

When they approached him about leaving, he refused. They realized their weirdo roommate had a deadly weapon in his possession, and if they upset him, they felt that he would attack them. It would have been a bad idea to argue with a crazy person, so the two women packed their bags and moved out instead.

Richard, on the other hand, was quite happy to be alone. His obsession with blood and human anatomy was getting more intense, and he could no longer keep living with a lack of blood.

When the time came for the rent to be paid, Richard found himself in trouble. The money he had received from his father and what he made from his occasional odd jobs was not enough to cover the rent and bills, so when the brother of one of his former roommates moved in, he knew he had to be less hostile.

Unfortunately, Richard's idea of "less hostile" was not exactly pleasant, either. Upon finding out that his new roommate and his friends had a rock band, Richard insisted on joining them. When the men came over to practice their instruments, he often showed up with bongo drums. While they tried to make music, Richard banged on without rhythm and sang loudly and off-key.

This new roommate was far less patient with Richard than his sister had been, and managed to kick him out.

Homeless again, Richard returned to live with his parents. They had believed that their son had been attending classes, and realizing he had dropped out dismayed them. Still, he was their son—and he needed help.

Richard was growing more resentful of them with each passing day. He believed that Beatrice was trying to poison him and control his mind, giving him disturbing, delusional thoughts.

He decorated the walls of his room with pictures of human hearts he cut out of anatomy books. It seemed his desire for blood could never be satisfied. Eventually, he could no longer think of anything else.

He needed blood, and he was going to get it by any means necessary.

IV

The Slow Descent

IN LATE 1971, RICHARD CHASE FOUND HIMSELF having to move back in with his parents after his failed attempt to live an independent life. Unfortunately, while he had been away, the Chase parents' marriage reached its breaking point, and the two separated. Richard returned to a home on Montclaire Street without his father.

Richard's life continued in its downward spiral. With his parents providing for him, he saw no need for full-time employment. On occasion, he would work odd jobs, but his eccentric behavior and drug addiction made it impossible for him to keep one for more than a few days. When he ended up with over five hundred dollars' worth of parking tickets, he continued to drive around, unconcerned with the legal consequences. It was his mother Beatrice who paid all his fines, but even so, Richard lost his license and sold his Volkswagen for a motorcycle.

In 1972, Richard left on a two-week trip to Utah accompanied only by his dogs: a small white one named Sabbath and a German Shepherd named Heavy. It is unclear what he did during this time, only that at some point he was arrested for, among other things, more traffic violations. His car was impounded, and Sabbath and Heavy were taken away and put in a shelter temporarily.

Once again, Beatrice bailed him out and brought him home, but she soon noticed that something about her son had changed while he was away.

He was just as paranoid and antsy as ever, but now he was constantly plagued by increasingly bizarre beliefs. According to Richard, something had happened in his cell that would affect him for the rest of his life. He told his mother that the police "poisoned" him, or "asphyxiated him in some way" that made him severely physically sick. In addition to not having enough blood, Richard believed that his body was rapidly deteriorating, that his stomach "was on backward," and that his heart would occasionally stop beating.

From this point forward, Richard began to suffer from what Beatrice called "fits." He was constantly agitated and would beat his feet against the walls of their home. It soon got so bad that his ability to speak deteriorated, and for some time, he even lost the ability to write his own name. The few times when Richard could talk, he would argue with his mother, and sometimes their fights turned physical. She then sent him to live with his father.

Richard's father did not want to give up on his son, who he believed was just misguided. While the elder Richard was doing home renovations, the younger man helped out, and even when working alone, he proved to be a competent handyman. Still, Richard refused to get a job, saying he was still too weak from an illness that left his entire body numb. This caused the two men to constantly argue, and eventually, Richard returned to live with his mother and sister.

His sister Pamela was shocked at how skinny her older brother had become. She thought he looked "spooky" and was increasingly disturbed by his actions. He was quick to anger and frequently threw violent tantrums. On one occasion, he got into an argument with his mother and attacked her while she tried to call the police, hitting her over the head with the phone. He jumped over the fence and ran away when he realized the police were coming, but was quickly caught and brought back. Beatrice, always the more lenient one, declined to press charges against her son.

As forgiving as Beatrice was, even she had reached her limit. Stress from dealing with Richard, as well as the aftermath of her divorce, caused her to reach out to her mother, Holly Neese, for help.

He was sent down to Los Angeles to live with his grandmother and got a job as a school bus driver for developmentally disabled children under his uncle.

Disorganized and messy, Richard performed poorly at his job. He never cleaned the bus or did any maintenance. The bus was constantly low on oil. He never washed his clothes or his hands and was always nervous. He was fired after about a year. It was the longest he would hold a job.

Unemployed again, he spent days sleeping and was only active at night, making all kinds of strange noises. Fed up with his eccentricities, Holly sent her grandson back to Sacramento around Christmas time.

It was a terrible holiday. With his parents divorced, the family was far from festive. Having to divide his time between the two made Richard tense. Though it would be some time before anyone could determine what was wrong with him, Richard was deeply suffering the effects of a severe mental illness. He felt alienated and alone, and more than anything wanted some relief from the pain he was in.

Little could anyone expect the extremes he would soon go to alleviate that pain.

V

The Party

DESPITE HIS WORSENING MENTAL ILLNESS, Richard would sometimes go through periods where his condition seemed to improve. After coming back to live with his mother after spending a year as a school bus driver in Los Angeles, his strange behaviors mellowed out for some time, and he became more social. Not only had he expressed interest in getting a job, but he had also started going out with friends again.

But like every bright spot of Chase's life, these hopeful days did not last long.

In early 1973, he got a job at a local paint store. Just a little over a week later, he quit. He had made enough money to buy something he had been eyeing for a while now—a .22-caliber pistol.

On April 22nd, he attended a small party at the apartment of one of his friends. Richard stood at the sidelines, drinking out of a brown paper bag. He spotted a young woman, who was the girlfriend of one of the men at the party. He watched her closely, waiting for the right chance to approach her. When the other men went out to purchase more alcohol, he and the woman were left alone together.

He made his move. His erectile dysfunction had kept him from ever knowing a woman sexually, but that did not mean he did not desire them. He was fascinated by the human body, particularly those of women. With no one to stop him, he grabbed hold of the woman and began to fondle and grope her breasts.

Startled, the woman stepped back. She told him to stop, but he ignored her pleas. As the woman hurried out of the room, Richard followed closely behind. It was clear to her what he wanted, and she knew he would not stop until he got it. A feeling of terror came over her.

Luckily for her, her boyfriend and the other men soon returned to the apartment. She explained what he had done to her, and the men, angered, demanded that Richard leave.

Richard's violent temper flared. He was practically screaming when he said nobody had the right to tell him what he could or could not do. If he was going to leave, it would only be because he wanted to. Nobody could force him to do anything.

Richard and the other men argued violently, and finally, after an hour, it seemed that Chase had had enough. Still fuming, he left the apartment.

Though the mood had been soured, the party resumed. Not long after, however, Richard was back looking for a pack of cigarettes he had left behind. As soon as he was inside the apartment, Richard became physically hostile. A fistfight broke out, and while the men attempted to subdue Richard, the small handgun fell out of his pocket and on the floor—right beyond his reach. Before Richard could grab his weapon, another man threw it in the bedroom.

Richard dared them to call the police, stating he was not afraid. The police arrived and took him away. He spent the night in county jail, was charged with a misdemeanor, and fined $50.

The next day, his father picked him up. As he always did whenever he got in trouble, Richard vehemently denied he had done anything wrong. He also claimed the police had been violent and seriously injured him. He wanted to sue, but his father managed to talk him out of it.

Unsure of how to handle their son, the Chase parents sent him back to live with his grandmother, Holly, in Los Angeles.

It was a trip that Holly Neese would never forget.

VI

You're A Good Boy, Richard

HOLLY COULD NOT BELIEVE THAT THIS WAS HER grandson. The last time he had come to stay with her, he was unkempt, lazy, and irresponsible. In less than a year, he had somehow gotten even worse. He was shockingly thin, as though he had stopped eating almost entirely. His long hair was matted and greasy, and he had not shaved his beard in quite some time. A foul odor followed him wherever he went.

He made no effort to find a job. He spent all his time inside, sleeping during the day, and making all sorts of loud noises at night. When asked what he was up to, he claimed to have been building something for his car. This resulted in Richard blowing out the electricity in Holly's living room and bathroom. The house was covered in newspapers that he would pull apart and leave on the floor.

Holly had a feeling that life with Richard was only going to get more unsettling.

Richard repeatedly told his grandmother that he was sick, but he could never quite specify with what. He was plagued by constant headaches, as well as a mysterious new pain in his leg. Believing that his illness was caused by a vitamin deficiency, he took to wrapping his head with a towel filled with orange slices. He explained that the nutrients from the fruit could seep into his head. When that did not work, he would stand on his head in the corner of his room to try and get the blood flowing back to his brain.

During this time, a disturbing new symptom of Richard's untreated mental illness began to show. One night, Holly overheard Richard having a conversation with someone. But nobody had come over. Was he talking to himself?

"Richard, you're a good boy, aren't you?" he asked himself. "Yes, you're a good boy."

Holly reached her limit when she found out that her mentally-ill grandson had purchased the .22-caliber handgun. Disturbed, Holly sent him back to Sacramento in July, just two months after he arrived.

He went back to live with his father at his house on Valkyrie Way. The elder Richard was not happy with his son. While Beatrice tried to be understanding of her son and his obvious mental illness, his father believed he was simply lazy and misguided. Now that he was 23 years old, it was due time that he man up and get a job.

The two men constantly bickered, sometimes even coming to blows. The resulting tension caused Richard to move back in with his mother, though, according to neighbors, it was not uncommon to see Richard standing in the middle of the driveway at Valkyrie Way, staring blankly at his father's house.

Living with Beatrice again was not much easier. His mother and sister had become afraid of him due to his violent outbursts and strange behavior. Even so, Beatrice was committed to helping her son.

Richard was still convinced he was very sick and begged his mother to take him to the doctor. Beatrice resisted, and on one occasion, he called the fire department, telling the operator that he was suffering from cardiac arrest. When the fire trucks and ambulance arrived, they realized that Richard was perfectly fine and refused to treat him. One paramedic, however, sensed that there was more going on than a simple lie. Despite all the evidence to the contrary, Richard genuinely believed he was going to die. Before they left, the paramedic suggested that Beatrice take her son to the hospital anyway.

On December 1st, 1973, Richard was admitted to the American River Hospital. When physician Doctor Irwin Lyons arrived, he gave a list of puzzling ailments: his heart had stopped beating and his blood stopped flowing, his kidneys stopped working, he had a persistent stomach ache and hernia, and somebody had "stolen" his pulmonary artery.

Tests revealed that there was nothing medically wrong with him, but this did not satisfy Richard. Dr. Lyons, on the other hand, began to suspect that this filthy, wild-eyed, and delusional young man was indeed unwell, but with an illness of the mind. When Richard was asked if he heard voices or had experienced hallucinations, he claimed he hadn't.

Then Richard claimed he was suffering from a brain aneurysm and ought to be placed in the intensive care unit. He did not want to answer any more questions about his sanity. He understood the human body just as well as any doctor because he often read articles in *Grey's Anatomy* about the heart, lungs, and stomach.

Richard's wild claims only further convinced the physician that he was mentally ill. Dr. Lyons thought he was likely suffering from "chronic acute paranoid schizophrenia." It made sense, given not only his disorganized lifestyle and odd beliefs, but also because 23-year-old Richard was at the prime age for schizophrenia to develop. In men, the onset of schizophrenic symptoms starts typically around late teens to early twenties.

However, given Richard's chronic drug use, Dr. Lyons also had to consider if these symptoms were instead the result of toxic psychosis. It was the better of two possible diagnoses since it was temporary, but it still required that Richard be held for at least 72 hours for observation in the psychiatric ward.

Unaware of Richard's violent behavior, the medical staff did not place him under careful confinement, and he soon left the hospital without permission. Beatrice brought him back but did not let him stay. She claimed that somebody had been bothering Richard and she would deal with his problems at home. When the staff tried to argue, she became hostile and provocative. Lyons referred to her as "the so-called schizophrenic mother."

This was far from the end of Richard's supposed illnesses. Throughout the next few years, Beatrice took him to a number of different doctors, one of which took a brain scan and electrocardiogram. Once again, there was nothing physically wrong with him, though Richard continued to say that his heart had stopped.

In 1976, the same doctor recommended Richard for welfare because his neurosis made it impossible for him to hold a job. He was also given an oxygen tank, likely as a treatment for his anxiety.

After this, Richard went through another phase where he seemed to improve. He started taking better care of himself by exercising and eating better, resulting in him putting about 20 pounds on his emaciated frame. This hopeful period only lasted a few months because Richard once again began to abuse illegal drugs, triggering his psychotic symptoms. But this time, he would reach a new low and was more violent than ever.

He terrorized his mother and sister. On more than one occasion, his sister, Pamela, fled from the house during his tirades. Beatrice also ran away in fear as he destroyed everything inside the home. He slapped his mother so hard that he knocked her to the ground. He kicked holes in the walls, broke windows, and knocked doors off their hinges. When Beatrice tried to call Richard Sr. for help, he arrived to find Richard pulling the phone and all its wires out from the wall.

He was also engaging in one-sided conversations with somebody who wasn't there. Beatrice overheard him repeating the same phrases: "Oh, shut up," or "I'm not going to do it." She initially thought that Richard was talking to her and would respond, though each time he would insist he was speaking to someone else.

Richard believed that his mother was controlling his mind and trying to poison him, so he stopped eating food prepared by her. The milk began to taste strange, and when Pamela tasted it, she realized her brother would flavor his milk with dish soap. Richard then claimed Pamela was trying to control him, too.

The stress of the situation made Beatrice's own mental disturbances rise to the surface. Upon noticing that her son tended to have his most violent episodes after speaking with Richard Sr. on the phone, she became convinced that her ex-husband was ordering Richard to break things and attack her.

One of Richard's most disturbing behaviors reappeared when he picked up his childhood hobby of torturing animals again. Using a pocket knife, he would poke and cut the paws of the family dog. Later, he grabbed the dog and held it by the snout, squeezing hard. The dog could not escape from his painful grip, and Richard held on until that part of the dog's skull almost cracked. For some time after this, the dog struggled to eat solid food.

Beatrice once again had enough. After another incident where she and Pamela had to flee their home, she knew she could not keep living with her son like this. Despite her own delusions, she called her ex-husband, and the elder Richard came down to try to stop the younger man. Paranoid and enraged, Richard got into a fistfight with his father outside his mother's home.

Both parents were at a loss of how to handle Richard. Desperate and exhausted, they did something that would be considered unthinkable today.

Together, they searched for an apartment for Richard to live in—on his own. He would be entirely unsupervised. Now he would be free to fulfill whatever dark desire he had.

VII

Dracula

RICHARD PEDALED HIS BIKE DOWN THE LONG road. He was coming home from a trip he had taken dozens of times in the short period since he had started living alone. Increasingly reclusive and socially distant, these ventures to the local rabbit farm at Rio Linda were one of his most frequent outings.

When he arrived at his new apartment on Cannon Street, he took the cage off his bike and headed inside. He placed it down beside the rest. His place was full of rabbits, and he made sure to restock once they ran out. He could not let himself run out of food, after all.

From a cage, he took out a rabbit and pinned it down on the table. It would not struggle for long. Richard took his knife and cut the animal open. As the blood seeped out of the carcass, he placed his face to its gaping wound and drank from it. Then he bit into its raw flesh and ate the oozing viscera.

It was not his preferred method of eating. He had a way that was much more efficient. He brought what was left of the rabbit to his blender, still stained from all the ones that came before it. Scooping out the remaining blood and organs, he put them in a blender until they were a thick, warm sludge. Richard would then drink them like a smoothie. Sometimes, he even mixed the stuff with Coca-Cola for a more palatable taste.

Richard cleaned up. His father would likely be arriving soon. Often, usually once a week, his father visited Richard to bring him groceries, and the two would play cards or chess. Despite everything that had happened, the elder Richard did not want his son to become lonely. It seemed his friends never hung out with Richard anymore, as they were off-put by his weirdness.

The older man arrived. He quickly took notice of the cages and asked Richard what he was doing with all these animals. Richard replied that he was eating them. It was the truth, though he was sure to leave out *how* he ate them.

It was an unusual answer, though compared to the other things his son did, it was nothing alarming. Richard's father was satisfied and did not bring the matter up again. He was content that Richard was at least eating and taking care of himself, even if he had a strange way of doing it.

They played chess and had a nice time. Richard seemed calmer these days, almost normal. His father was relieved that Richard had stopped mentioning his impossible illnesses. Though he was still unkempt and jobless, his father hoped that his son was slowly becoming more independent.

When the elder Richard stopped for another visit the following day, he assumed all was normal—as normal as it ever got with Richard. When he came back later in the day, he was surprised to see the apartment's door wide open. As he approached, he was suddenly hit by a disgusting smell. He had gotten used to his son's foul odor, but this was something different. The overwhelming stink of blood and vomit turned his stomach.

He hurried inside and found his son, stripped down to his underwear, sitting on the couch. All the color had drained from his face, leaving him a ghastly pale. All around him, the place was covered with his vomit. It was clear that he had somehow quickly become violently ill in the short time since his father last saw him.

When his father asked what was wrong, Richard responded that he had bought a "bad" rabbit and got food poisoning when he tried to eat it. Alarmed, he quickly got Richard to his car and took him to the emergency room at the Sacramento Community Clinic. By the time he was admitted, Richard was in shock and getting worse.

Richard's vital signs revealed that he was indeed very sick, but not with food poisoning. The attending physician believed that his symptoms were more in line with blood poisoning and that he could be going into septic shock. Septic shock, the doctor told Richard, was not caused by eating any part of a diseased animal. It was far more likely that he had gotten sick from dirty needles, though the doctor noticed that Richard's skinny arms lacked the tracks often seen on drug addicts.

It had to have been because of the rabbit he ate, Richard insisted. He told the doctor that this particular rabbit had eaten battery acid, and when he ate it, the battery acid corroded the walls of his stomach and seeped into his flesh.

This made the doctor suspicious.

Richard asked to be moved to another ward because he was afraid of contracting a disease from the other patients. He was terrified of contamination. Then he began insisting that his blood pressure was zero because his blood was turning into dust. He insisted his circulatory system was no longer working and causing his body to fall apart. The doctor talked to Richard's parents and learned he had an extensive history of drug use, including marijuana, LSD, narcotics, and more.

It was soon revealed that Richard didn't just drink the rabbit's blood; he was injecting himself with it. He believed his own supply was critically low, and he had been trying to replenish it with the animal's blood.

After running a few more tests on his heart and lungs, the doctor's suspicions were confirmed: he was dealing with a paranoid schizophrenic who was also suffering from somatic delusions. As soon as Richard recovered from the blood poisoning, he was to be transferred to the psychiatric ward of the American River Hospital and held for at least 14 days.

Richard protested. He claimed he was perfectly sane and only needed treatment for food poisoning. He again became violent and unreasonable at being forced to do something he did not want to. When he was told that police or hospital staff would simply bring him back if he tried to leave the hospital, Richard wanted to speak to a lawyer.

He was admitted to the psychiatric ward on April 28th, 1976, and two days later, he tried to run out the door. Hospital staff chased after him and managed to catch him, but Richard struggled until he broke free. The next day, his father brought him back.

Doctor Frank Harper, the admitting physician at the American River Hospital, noted that while Richard was openly hostile, he was still "oriented to time, place, and person" and "complained about heart weakness." Hospital staff claimed he was almost completely nonverbal.

It was clear that Richard needed more intensive care than the American River Hospital could provide, so he was transferred on May 19th to Beverly Manor, a facility that specializes in mental health. Michael Buckley, another doctor, wrote in his report that Richard had been entirely uncooperative with treatment and was again diagnosed with paranoid schizophrenia.

Richard had trouble adjusting from the moment he entered Beverly Manor. When he arrived, he was visibly nervous, and still claimed he was only there because of food poisoning. He continued to tell the staff that he was sane and needed help for his physical symptoms instead and that he could only be cured with blood. When the staff tried to get him to participate in the hospital's exercise classes or group therapy, he declined. He continued to withdraw further and would refuse to socialize with anyone.

Slowly, however, Richard began to open up and talk with other patients. He started participating in groups and started playing basketball with the others. Doctors hoped this increased socialization meant his condition was improving, but while the medication he was prescribed eased his hostility and paranoia, he still openly spoke about how he enjoyed consuming blood. His descriptions of how he would eat animals raw disturbed patients and staff alike. These obsessions gained him the nickname "Dracula"; one he would carry long after he left Beverly Manor.

His troubling behavior worsened after one of the housekeepers began to suspect that Richard was still killing animals right in the hospital itself. During their rounds one day, the housekeeper passed by Richard's room and noticed the headless corpses of two small birds on the floor. Cautiously, they opened the door to check on Richard.

The patient turned around with big, wild eyes, blood dripped from his mouth and down his chin, staining the front of his shirt a deep, dark red.

The housekeeper asked what happened. Richard replied that he cut himself while shaving.

This was not the only time he had been caught killing birds. A hospital orderly found a dead bird in the wastebasket in Richard's room. Later, the staff found Richard crouched in the bushes. All around him were the feathers he tore off an unlucky bird, and its blood smeared on his face.

Doctors realized the anti-psychotic medication they had put him on was proving to be ineffective. The very worst of his symptoms had not improved at all, and everyone was afraid of him. It was getting so bad that two nurses quit after having to work with him.

Meanwhile, the question of what to do with Richard was still up in the air. Since his mental illness made it impossible for him to hold a job, Richard's parents would have to continue to support him, but the issue went deeper than just money. Richard Narver of the Sacramento Public Guardian's Office decided the best course of action would be for Richard's parents to be appointed as his conservators.

A conservatorship is a type of legal guardianship mostly given for disabled adults. As their son's conservators, Richard Sr. and Beatrice were given the authority to decide where Richard would live as well as manage his relationships and finances.

Richard himself did not argue against the conservatorship, and after a few months, his condition greatly improved. By September of 1976, it was decided that he was at last well enough to be discharged. His doctor believed that Richard had developed good socialization skills, was thinking clearer, and gained a more realistic view of his health issues during his stay at Beverly Manor, but the staff had a much different view.

Upon hearing that the blood-obsessed animal killer was going to be released back into society, they reportedly "raised hell" about it. Having dealt with Richard on a daily basis, they knew that not only was he still very sick, but that he was likely a danger to others. The staff claimed that the real reason he was being discharged was that the facility was overcrowded.

On September 29th, 1976, against the pleas of the hospital staff, Richard Chase was set free into the world again.

VIII

The Zombie

BEATRICE CHASE DROPPED OFF A BAG OF groceries at apartment number 12 at the Watt Avenue Complex. This was a chore she was used to, but it was easier now that she had help. Every month, her son would get a little over $200 from Social Security, and that would pay for his rent and utilities. She and her ex-husband took care of everything else.

It had been a while since Richard had complained to her about any strange illnesses. In fact, he seemed the most normal he had ever been since his release from Beverly Manor. For the first time in years, he was easy to manage. By 1977, when it came time to decide if they wanted to renew their conservatorship over him, they decided that it was no longer necessary.

Newly independent, the now 27-year-old Richard moved out of his apartment and decided to travel across the country. With only about a thousand dollars of money he had saved up from his welfare payments, he headed to Washington, D.C. Eighteen days later, he came back with a new car, a Ford Ranchero, that he bought in Steamboat Springs, Colorado.

After a brief stay with his mother and sister, Richard moved back to the Watt Avenue Complex, this time to apartment number 15. Beatrice continued to believe that Richard was doing well on his own, but when she went to visit again, she noticed the adverse effects of the medication he had been prescribed for his schizophrenia.

As schizophrenia was not as well understood back in the 70s, it was far more difficult to treat. Richard's medication eased his aggression and somatic delusions, but it also diminished his energy and vitality. Richard became constantly sluggish, almost "zombie-like," as his mother described him. This distressed Beatrice, and she figured she had to help her son.

Beatrice decided that Richard would be fine without his medication and slowly weaned him off of it.

For a while, he did seem to do just fine. Richard continued to go to his appointments with his new physician—until he abruptly stopped going after the second visit. He appeared to be in good health—until he was convinced that he was suffering from a blood clot in his brain that caused headaches. He appeared to have remained sociable and hung out with old friends from high school at the Country Club Lanes Bowling Alley—until he started ranting about UFOs and how a secret Nazi organization had been after him since he was a teenager.

Once again, he had begun taking illicit drugs. Some days he appeared more well-adjusted, spending time with his father without making any odd claims about his health. At other times, he would do seemingly nonsensical things such as subletting his apartment to strangers, only to call Richard Sr. to chase away the unwanted guests later.

By the time the next summer came around, Richard had begun to act more deranged than ever.

He once again began torturing the family's same German Shepherd, Heavy, whose snout he nearly broke before. According to Beatrice, Richard clearly gained some sort of sick pleasure from inflicting pain on the poor animal. In the summer of 1977, he killed both Heavy and Sabbath, the family's other dog. When confronted about this, he told his parents, "I had a right to do what I wanted to." as the dogs belonged to him.

Then one evening, Beatrice heard a loud bang right outside her door. She tried to ignore it. She figured it was Richard, and after watching him descend back into madness, she could not bear to see him.

Still, the knocks persisted.

That was when she heard a gunshot. Frightened, she went to check her front door. There, at her doorway, she saw her son covered in blood. In one hand, he held a rifle, and in the other, he held her cat by its tail. It was dead. He had shot it once through the head. Its brains were splattered all over her front porch.

Beatrice watched as he threw the cat's corpse to the ground. He got down on his knees and flipped the animal on its back. He tore the skin of its stomach open as easily as if it were made out of wet paper and reached inside the hole he had made and smeared the blood all over his face as he shrieked. Speechless and afraid, his mother shut the door.

She, at last, had enough. She knew she could not handle her son anymore.

Richard's paranoia increased, and he stopped letting his family inside his apartment because he believed they were trying to poison him. In early 1977, he shaved his head down to the scalp and went to the doctor's office where he told a nurse that he was fatigued, unable to sleep, and wanted blood. When this bizarre request was denied, he left without issue, but returned several times. However, he seemed to be apprehensive during social situations, and would always leave once he saw the busy waiting room.

Richard was similarly a menace at the Watt Avenue Complex. One of his neighbors, Dawn Larson (though some reports give her name as Linda Dillon), often noticed the quiet, ungroomed young man. He was clearly weird, she thought. She sometimes saw him walking around the apartment complex dragging one foot behind him, his mouth hanging open. Once, he had even come inside her apartment uninvited and left when he saw other people inside.

He never spoke to her or anyone else, and visits from others seemed to be getting scarcer and scarcer. On more than one occasion, she witnessed him carrying dogs and cats into his apartment, despite the strict no-pets rule.

None of those animals were ever seen again.

Later, she would recall a frightening incident she had with Richard in early January 1978. On the day she was set to move out of the complex, she went to check her mail. At the long wall of mailboxes, she spotted Richard. He was muttering to himself, obviously highly upset at something.

"Do you have a cigarette?" he asked.

Dawn was startled, but she gave him a friendly smile and pulled out her pack. She handed one to him and turned to walk back home.

But Richard was not done with her yet. Before she could get away, he grabbed her, squeezing her shoulder so hard that it hurt. He turned her around and looked her all over. Despite his apparent aggression, she noticed that his face was completely blank.

"You got any more?" he demanded.

Dawn did not protest. She handed him the entire pack and fled. There was never a better time to move away than now. Other neighbors, believing that Richard posed a threat to their safety and annoyed with his noisiness, also left the complex not long after.

He began carrying his gun with him everywhere, even walking around the apartment complex with his rifle in hand. When his worried neighbors complained to the landlord, Richard was told to cover his weapon up with a blanket. He obeyed.

Little did anyone know that soon, one of Richard's behaviors would build up to something far more disturbing.

IX

I'd Rather Be Flying

THE AUGUST HEAT WAS RELENTLESS. THE SUN beat down on the desert sands, making the land appear more desolate than usual. Despite the lake that lay beyond the stretch of dry land, it was rare to see anyone who was not from the area. Pyramid Lake, part of Nevada's vast Walker River Reservation, was populated mostly by the members of the Paiute Indian tribe.

A call came on the radio about a wanderer who abandoned his truck on the shore of the lake, accompanied only by a dog. He was spotted by Carman Tobey Sr., who immediately called the police. This news troubled Charles O'Brien, an officer with the Bureau of

Indian Affairs. Everyone knew the desert was dangerous, but for an outsider unfamiliar with the land, it could be downright deadly.

O'Brien, joined by other officers as well as Tribal police, began their search, and before long, they located the vehicle in question. It was a silver 1966 Ford Ranchero stuck deep within the sand. The license plate, from Florida, expired. On the front bumper was a sticker that read: "I'd Rather Be Flying!" O'Brien opened the door and found a 30/30 lever-action Marlin rifle and a .22-caliber semiautomatic rifle. Both weapons were loaded and covered with blood.

Alongside the weapons was a pile of men's clothing and a pair of tennis shoes also stained with blood. O'Brien then spotted a white bucket on the floor of the cab. He looked into it and was met with a horrifying sight: an entire liver sitting in a pool of blood.

He recoiled. This organ, he knew, was much too big to belong to a small animal. It could very well have been inside a human being at one point.

Something was very wrong. They needed to find this missing person, and fast.

They set out quickly. With a four-wheel-drive vehicle and powerful binoculars, they scanned the surrounding area until, at last, they found something. About a mile south, a man sat on a small, rocky cliff over the desert shrub-land. He was completely naked, and he was covered in blood.

From his place on the cliff, the man could see them headed their way. He hurried down and, undeterred by the blazingly hot sand against his bare feet, sprinted away. But he was no match for the officers in their four-wheel drive, and before long, he was in custody.

The officers brought him back to his pickup truck. The sight of him was alarming. He had intentionally smeared blood across his face and chest. It was in his long hair, making it matted and sticky. He was a sickly sort of pale, no doubt caused in part by a lack of nutrition. This man, nearly six feet tall, was so thin it was scary.

What sort of person was this, and more importantly, where did all this blood come from?

The man gave his name. Richard Trenton Chase. He had come all the way from Sacramento. When asked where the blood was from, Richard replied that the blood was his. It was seeping out of his skin and it would not stop. The dog was nowhere to be found. He had a knife sheath on him, but the knife was missing.

He had only come to look around, Richard said. He abandoned his truck after it had gotten stuck in the sand. He was not up to anything nefarious.

The officers ordered Richard to put his clothing on. They took a more careful look at his body and noticed that the blood was not just smeared over his front; it was everywhere on him. His body hair was encrusted with it. It was even smeared under his armpits.

O'Brien again asked where the blood had really come from. Now Richard said it was from a deer he had shot in Colorado back in May. Three months previously. An obvious lie.

They had to take this man in for questioning. Upon hearing that he was going to be taken to the Washoe County Jail in Reno, he became belligerent. Officers called the U.S. Deputy Attorney, who ordered for him to be arrested for federal gun law violations. Richard resisted aggressively to the point where the officers had to restrain him as they drove off with him. His truck was then impounded due to the expired vehicle registration number.

Richard called his mother, telling her that there had been a mix-up with the police and that he had only killed rabbits. A few days later, Richard Sr. drove to Sparks, Nevada, to take Richard home. After a couple of attempts, he managed to get his truck back by showing proof of ownership.

Just four days later, lab tests on the liver and blood found in the bucket revealed that they had belonged to a cow. Ray Pike, the U.S. Deputy Attorney who had ordered his arrest, no longer wanted to prosecute, and all of the charges were dropped. Richard headed home to Sacramento.

X

The First Kill

BACK IN HIS APARTMENT, HIS NEED FOR BLOOD only intensified as the year went on. On October 1st, 1977, Richard went to the local SPCA and purchased a dog for $15.99. Ten days later, he went back and bought another. When he was through with those, he answered a newspaper ad from a woman named Alane Maier, advertising puppies for $20.

When he arrived to meet Alane, she immediately noticed that the dogs cowered at the sight of him, as though they could somehow suspect the gruesome fate they would soon meet, though she would later state that Richard had behaved perfectly normal. Richard tried to haggle her for a lower price, but Alane refused. He paid $25 and took the dog home, where police would ultimately find its tags.

In mid-November, Daniel Owens came home to find Richard staring into his yard from beyond the fence. Richard told the man that he was a breeder and was responding to an ad Daniel had placed in the local paper selling Labrador puppies for $10 each. Daniel sold him two puppies for a two-for-one price, though he found it strange that a breeder would pay no attention to the dogs he chose.

Sometime later, Richard stole a dog from the Sudseths, a family who lived close by his apartment complex. Since he paid close attention to the newspaper, he soon saw a missing dog notice in the newspaper. He called the family and, in a shrill, high-pitched, nearly incoherent voice, taunted them. He claimed he knew exactly what had happened to their lost puppy and told them about it in graphic detail. The distraught daughter handed the phone to her father, who demanded to know the caller's name. Richard immediately hung up.

He later attempted to steal a rather large dog, a Saint Bernard, from Joann Hoey's home, though he was caught by a neighbor. He tried again but was caught by Joann herself. She asked what he wanted, and Richard left without saying anything. This lucky dog managed to avoid the horrific end the other dogs met at Richard's hands.

Richard would take the dogs home to his apartment, kill them, and hang their bodies in order to drain the blood. He drank the blood and ate their flesh and organs raw.

Then December came along with another one of Richard's hopeful periods. It had been an incredibly tense year, but Richard finally seemed to be getting his life back together and spoke about possibly getting a job. Richard's father, pleased with his son's improvement, took him shopping and let him pick out his own Christmas present, an orange ski parka.

Around this time, Richard went to a sporting goods store and bought his own present: a new gun. He was asked a series of standard questions, including if he had a history of mental health issues or had ever been committed to a psychiatric hospital, to which Richard replied that he had not. Store policy stated that he could not take the gun home right away and had to wait. In the meantime, Richard called his mother to ask her to buy a gun holster for him. Beatrice declined, and the conversation ended there.

The Chase family was carefully optimistic that Christmas. Holly, the grandmother, came up from Los Angeles to visit for the holiday and was surprised to see her grandson looking better than he had in a long time. Richard was clean, groomed, and wearing new clothes. He even seemed to show consideration for others, something that was considered unusual for him. He even asked how Holly's dog was doing. So impressed was Holly that she gave Richard $10 before she left.

Beatrice also took her son Christmas shopping and went out to dinner with him. When finally Christmas came, she arrived at his apartment with several gifts. Richard was reportedly surprised and delighted by this. These happy moments, unfortunately, were as short-lived as the ones before.

According to Beatrice, while Richard enjoyed his gifts, what he wanted was to spend time with the family during the holiday. However, after seeing what he had done to her cat, Beatrice was still hesitant to allow him back to her home. After killing the family dogs, Pamela expressed her fear of her brother and said she did not want him around anymore. After being told he was not invited, Richard repeatedly called, begging to join the family, but his mother would not change her mind.

This rejection, Richard would later recall, was what made him finally snap. On December 26th, he purchased an extra box of ammunition, and three days later, he was ready to move up from killing animals to killing people.

Richard drove around until he reached Robertson Avenue, a suburb in Sacramento's East Side. He cared little about who his target was. This was only a warm-up for the crimes that were soon to come. All he wanted was to kill and get a feeling for what it was like to end the life of a human being.

Outside his window, he spotted a family that had just returned home from a shopping trip. Richard drove closer and watched as the husband and wife unloaded groceries from their car. The wife went inside the house. The husband remained outside, getting the last two bags from the trunk. Here, at last, was his chance.

Without stopping, Richard fired, and the man, 51-year-old Ambrose Griffin, collapsed to the ground.

As Richard drove off, Ambrose's wife, Carol Griffin, ran outside when she heard her husband give a short, pained yell. The sight of Ambrose lying on the ground made her scream and cry. Carol turned and shouted for their two sons still in the house to call for help. Concerned neighbors came outside and watched her kneel beside her husband, telling them that he was at the perfect age for a heart attack.

It was only when the paramedics arrived that Carol learned the awful truth. Her beloved husband was dead—and he had been murdered in a drive-by shooting.

Sergeant Don Habecker and Detective Fred Homen from the Sacramento County's Sheriff's Department's Homicide Unit were promptly assigned to the case, but decided to wait until the next morning to question the family. Understandably, they were still at the hospital with Ambrose's body, mourning and in shock. A Catholic priest had joined them.

Carol spoke with the police early the following day. The more she spoke with them, the clearer her memories of the incident became. When she was still inside the house, she heard two popping noises, though she was not sure what they were at the time. She was far more concerned with what was happening to her husband. These sounds, they all realized, were from the murder weapon.

Other than this, there was nothing else for the investigation to go on. It was hard enough dealing with the swell of homicide cases that had been plaguing the area in recent times, but this one had been completely random. There was seemingly no pattern or motivation.

Ambrose Griffin, an engineer with the Federal Bureau of Land Management, had no enemies. He was a man that had a comfortable sort of averageness to him; he was a friendly, easygoing sort of person who loved his family. He worked in an office where his fellow employees liked him. What reason could anyone have to murder him in cold blood?

A possible lead came when Bob, the younger of Ambrose's two sons, called the police to report a suspicious man that his brother, Rick, had seen carrying a rifle near their home. They assumed it was the culprit, and the sight of him walking free so soon after their father's death enraged them. The brothers followed the man and cornered him. That was where they were when the police found them.

When the police questioned this man, they inspected his rifle and found it could not have been their murder weapon. This was a 30/30-caliber hunting rifle, and Ambrose had been killed by a .22-caliber pistol. The man, employed at a nearby gas station, was also not in the area when the shooting happened. It was not possible that this man was their suspect.

Richard, it seemed, was getting away with murder.

XI

The Next Sightings

THE GRIFFIN INVESTIGATION HAD GROUND TO A halt before it ever really started. Though locals called in with tips and theories, very few of them had any relevant information. Neighbors reported anyone who might have owned a gun as well as anyone they were not fond of, which ended up complicating matters even further. The wrong leads could have compromised the entire case, but with so little evidence to go on, the police had no choice but to listen to whatever information came their way.

The only consistent information involved the sighting of a suspicious tan or brown vehicle, but even then, nobody could agree on what kind of car it was.

The only thing that was clear was that Ambrose Griffin's murder had been entirely senseless. He had been the unfortunate victim of a thrill killer, in the wrong place at the wrong time.

At last, a witness with more information came forward—a 12-year-old in the seventh grade, though his mother was confident in his good character. An excellent and responsible student, the boy was never known to lie. It made the following story he gave feel much more urgent.

On the day Ambrose Griffin was killed, he was riding his bike when he went by a store on Marconi Avenue, a few blocks away from the crime scene. A brown Pontiac Trans Am drove by, the boy's favorite type of car, catching his attention. He stopped and watched the vehicle go by. He almost did not notice when the driver took his hands away from the steering wheel, pulled out a gun, and shot at him.

The shot missed, thankfully. It hit the window of the store instead, shattering glass. The boy fell off his bike and hit the ground. He was completely unharmed, but the near-miss left him shaky and afraid.

The boy had not seen much of the driver, only that he had been a brown-haired male likely in his early 20s who used some sort of snub-nosed handgun. It was an incredibly vague description, but coupled with the story about the brown Trans Am, it was by far the best lead the police had. If only the boy had seen more...

In the 1970s, law enforcement began using hypnosis as a method of getting forgotten information out of the subconscious minds of their witnesses. It wasn't an exact science; some courts believed that police pressure could "influence" witnesses' memories, rendering their testimony unreliable. Courts set strict guidelines when the practice was involved: hypnosis sessions had to be witnessed, videotaped, and conducted by a mental health professional. In the boy's case, one of his parents needed to be present.

Two days after his first interview, the boy met with Leroy Wolter, a Ph.D. in hypnosis in the Sherriff's Department. The boy responded well to the session and recalled a few more important details about the car and its driver. Among the most important was the license plate number: 219EEP.

Using the Department of Motor Vehicle's computers, the detectives tried to locate the suspicious car. Unfortunately, even after running 219EEP and similar numbers through the database, the search once again hit a wall. There were no registered Trans Am owners within the Sacramento area. Two Pontiacs with vaguely similar numbers were not brown or tan, nor were they Trans Ams.

After that, there was no more helpful information that the boy could provide, and for several days, the case went cold.

On January 9th, 1978, a more promising lead surfaced. After a few fruitless days searching the area for clues, detectives came across a routine police report that had been filed on December 27th, 1977—two days before Ambrose Griffin was murdered. Dorothy Polenske, who lived on Lynn Avenue, a few blocks away from the Griffin house, reported a shot that had been fired into her home.

It happened at around six-thirty in the evening. Dorothy had just finished having dinner and was doing the dishes when she suddenly heard a sharp noise. The kitchen window broke, sending shards of sharp glass everywhere. Something fast and hot passed right above her head, piercing her thick hair bun. Cautiously, she touched her hair. She didn't find anything.

Since there were no injuries, the police report was brief, but Sergeant Habecker and Detective Homen thought the woman might have more details.

Dorothy was surprised when the police came to her home, but after hearing that there had been a shooting nearby, she was more than willing to tell them what she knew. Even though nearly a month had passed since the incident, the police still wanted to inspect her kitchen.

The two men looked through every inch of the kitchen for about 30 minutes until, at last, they found what they were searching for. Within one of the cupboards, hidden behind cups and dishes that were surprisingly still intact, was a single bullet embedded in the wood. They dug out the bullet, bagged it up, and brought it back to the crime lab for testing.

Not long after, criminalist Alan Gilmore called the man in charge of the investigation, Lieutenant Ray Biondi. He was more than happy to inform him that the bullet was indeed a match. It had come from the gun used to murder Ambrose Griffin.

At last, there was something solid to go on. But the harsh reality of the situation set in. Dorothy Polenske had no association with Ambrose Griffin, and like Ambrose, she had no known enemies.

They were dealing with a murderer who killed indiscriminately and randomly. There was no telling when they would kill again or who. All they knew was that a killer like this never stopped on their own.

Next time would be worse.

Meanwhile, Richard was relishing in his crime. On January 5th, 1978, he purchased a copy of *The Sacramento Bee* that featured an article about Ambrose Griffin's mysterious slaying, which he circled. It would later be discovered that Richard kept newspapers detailing his and other crimes as trophies and possibly sources of inspiration. On January 6th, he bought another paper and circled a mention of a knife-attack killing.

Not content with only murder, Richard began making all sorts of trouble in the area before his next killing. Paranoid, Richard went into the parking lot at the Watt Avenue Apartment Complex and set a bundle of newspapers on a shelf. He set the papers on fire and fled the scene, hoping that the flame would drive away the neighbors he was convinced had been spying on him. He strangely did not seem intent on actually harming anyone and knocked on the door of one of the apartments to alert the people inside. The fire was discovered and put out without issue. Luckily, perhaps as Richard had intended, nobody was hurt.

He began speaking with his mother again and visited her, finally allowed back into her house. Despite the bump their relationship had hit over the holidays, things seemed to be on the mend. He mentioned his desire to spend time outdoors, and they organized for him to go on a hiking trip with Richard Sr. later that month.

That same day, Richard broke the window of the Nelson family residence at 3040 Watt Avenue. He checked to see if anybody was home, and once he found that the place was empty, he crawled in through the broken window and set fire to the curtains before fleeing. By the time the fire department arrived, the flames had spread to the carpet and a speaker cabinet. Again, nobody was harmed.

These incidents of arson, bizarre and seemingly pointless as they were, proved to be building up to an even greater crime. Soon, Richard was going to do something that would shock Sacramento—and the world—for years to come.

XII

The Rampage Begins

A FEW DAYS AFTER HE TERRORIZED HIS neighbor, Dawn Larson, by the mailboxes, Richard was out to cause trouble just a short block away.

It was not yet ten in the morning when Jeanne Layton had been watching television and heard a noise in her yard. She went to investigate and spotted him coming toward the door of her house. He had given up on hygiene in the previous days, and his slovenly appearance worried her.

The housewife froze with fear when he reached the patio. She prayed that the door was locked. She watched as the doorknob turned slightly.

It did not open. Jeanne sighed with relief.

But the stranger was undeterred. Next, he decided to try the kitchen window, and Jeanne worked up the courage to follow him. Thankfully, all of the windows in the house were locked tight. Yet the man still wanted in and headed back to the patio.

Jeanne did not realize he had not left when she returned to the kitchen. She stood at the sink, trying to busy herself when she got the urge to look up. There he was, standing in front of the window, staring at her with wide, animal-like eyes. The strange, dirty man said nothing as he watched her. His gaunt face, pale and emotionless, did not match his eyes.

She recoiled, but at last, the man said something. Faintly, he muttered something under his breath that sounded like "excuse me." He turned, lit a cigarette, and left the yard.

Had this all been a misunderstanding, she wondered. She sat at the kitchen table, her heart still pounding. The ordeal had left her feeling shaky and unwell. She considered calling the police, but the more she thought about it, the more unreasonable the idea seemed. The guy had been a creep, sure, but it was not a crime to walk through someone's yard. It was likely that he was not from the area and had gotten lost looking for a friend's house.

Or at least that was what she hoped. She had no idea that a locked door was all that had kept her from death that day.

A half-hour later, Robert Edwards and his wife returned from a shopping trip to their home on 2929 Burnece Street. Right as they were about to unlock their front door, they heard the sound of someone walking through their house. That was alarming. Nobody had been home when they left.

Whoever was inside must have heard them because they immediately heard the unmistakable sound of footsteps running to the back of the house. A window opened and slammed shut.

A moment later, Robert spotted the intruder. A filthy, disheveled young man came out from behind the corner of the house. Angered, he commanded the other man to stop.

In response, the startled intruder cut past the couple and ran down the block. He was headed in the direction of the Watt Avenue Apartment Complex. Robert followed the man down the sidewalk. The stranger was fast, but with the streets largely empty of traffic at this hour, Robert had no trouble keeping sight of him, and soon, he nearly caught up. He was right within Robert's reach.

Unfortunately, Robert could only watch as the man slipped away. The intruder made a sudden sharp right turn. He rushed down a wide lawn and climbed over a wooden fence.

In vain, Robert shouted again for him to stop.

Right before the intruder jumped over the fence, he called back to Robert. "I'm just taking a shortcut!" he said, as though it had all just been a matter of miscommunication.

Exhausted and defeated, Robert gave up on trying to follow him. It was whatever had happened within their home that was more important. He headed back for Burnece Street and saw that in the short time he had been gone, law enforcement showed up in response to his wife's call for help. Because there had been several cops in the immediate area when the dispatcher alert came, there were more than a few of them who had shown up at the Edwards' home.

The police concluded that the intruder entered and escaped through the same back room window. He had clumsily left footprints in the soil. It was not much to go on, but they could photograph the crime scene and make plaster casts for the prints.

Meanwhile, Robert could only wonder what had gone on inside the house. The intruder had left the place an absolute mess. Closets and drawers were wide open. Piles of clothing were thrown across the floor. It was clear that the man had gone through every inch of the place, looking for anything he could steal and sell. Luckily, at the very least, it appeared that he had been unsuccessful in taking their cash and valuables. All of their rings had been placed inside one jewelry box; binoculars, a stethoscope, a cassette player, and even a decorative dagger had been packed into a cloth bag that the intruder left behind when he heard the couple coming home earlier than expected.

The criminal was, no doubt, a dirty, careless person. It was not the money he was after; it was the thrill of invading someone's private space, of making people helpless and afraid. He was the type of person who liked to be in control and got upset when he wasn't.

His idea of being in control was just as warped as the rest of his mind. That much was obvious. When Robert and Barbara went back into their house, they realized with horror that the intruder had been inside their child's bedroom. He had urinated inside the drawer, over the child's clothing, and had defecated on the bed.

Richard went on to commit his third act of terror before noon that same day.

Inside the Pantry Market, a grocery store within the Town and Country Village Shopping Center, Nancy Holden navigated her shopping cart through the aisles, unaware of the person following her. She only noticed him when he started walking directly toward her. The man looked oddly familiar, but she turned away from him anyway, not wanting to take any chances.

"Were you on the motorcycle when Curt was killed?" asked the man suddenly.

The strange question confused Nancy. How did this guy know the name of someone she had dated ten years ago? They were not even in a relationship anymore by the time Curt got in a motorcycle accident that ended his life. Who was this person, and why was he so curious?

The man came closer and repeated his question.

Nancy backed away a little. "Who are you?" she asked, barely able to get the words out.

"Rick," he responded.

"You're Rick Chase?" she asked.

Nancy took another look at him. Yes, that name was familiar. It took her a moment, but at last, she realized who it was standing before her. Richard Trenton Chase. They had gone to high school together, but he had been a few grades ahead of her. The only reason she really knew him was that her older sister dated him for a short period.

She thought back to that time. Was this man really Rick? He was a far cry from the well-groomed, intelligent young man she had known then. What on earth happened to him? She had heard rumors that his life fell apart after he got addicted to drugs, but she never suspected he had gotten this bad.

He had fallen hard. His pants and orange jacket were dirty with something she could not make out. There was so much grime beneath his fingernails that she could see it from where she stood. His hair was greasy and matted. His face was stained, and something yellow was encrusted around his lips. He had a rather strong, unpleasant smell to him.

"You're Nancy Westfall," he said, using her maiden name. He nodded and turned away for a moment before coming back.

Reluctantly, she stayed and talked with him for a bit. Richard was fidgety and awkward. She tried to ask him about how he was and what he had been up to in the years since he graduated, but he answered her questions with complete nonsense. It made Nancy feel incredibly uncomfortable.

She tried to excuse herself by telling him that she needed to finish shopping and hurried to a different aisle. Right when she thought she had gotten away from him, Richard appeared a second time. Anxiety made her heart sink.

Nancy decided to give up on the rest of her shopping. She needed to get away from him and fast. But when she got to the check-out, Richard was there, waiting for her.

"Where are you going in such a hurry?" he asked.

"I'm going to pay," she replied, trying her best to sound calm.

"Listen, I need a ride."

"Sorry," she said as fear gripped her. "I can't."

"I gotta get outta' here right away." Richard's voice was intense.

Nancy apologized, paid the cashier, and carried her groceries out the door as fast as she could. Richard was right behind her, buying a single can of orange soda. If she was going to escape him, she did not have much time.

"Wait!" she heard him shout as she ran to her car.

Nancy unlocked her car and threw the groceries on the back seat. She made sure all the doors were locked. Fear made it hard to get the key in the ignition. By the time she finally started up the engine, he had his hand on the door handle. He held on until Nancy backed up her vehicle and only let go when she sped off.

She had no idea how lucky she had gotten because, later that very same day, Richard's sadism would reach new heights.

XIII

A Nightmare of the Flesh

RICHARD'S FAMILY HAD NO IDEA JUST HOW BUSY he had been on the morning of January 23, 1978. They had reason to believe he was still doing well.

In the early hours of the same day that Richard terrorized Jeanne Layton, the Edwards, and Nancy Holden, he had gone hiking with his father to collect rocks. The two men had a nice time, enjoying each other's company, despite Richard's bad smell, as though they had decided to put the past behind them. Richard made no arguments or any strange claims. It was something they hoped to do again together.

Nobody had any idea that, in just a few short hours, Richard would commit his second murder.

After scaring Nancy Holden away, Richard walked out of the shopping center's parking lot and headed down the road. Eventually, he made it to Tioga Way, a neighborhood of modest track houses not too far from the Watt Avenue apartments. He carelessly walked across the porch of a resident who took notice of him, but Richard never stopped to look back.

He was too busy planning the terrible crime that was about to come.

He saw the house in the distance: 2360 Tioga Way. A blue van parked in the driveway indicated somebody was home. As he came closer, he could see that inside the house was a pretty young woman, and she was alone. It is believed that he first saw her at Pantry Market, where she had been to cash a check just over an hour previously.

Richard pulled out his gun, a .22-caliber semiautomatic handgun that had been perfectly concealed in a shoulder holster under his orange parka. He cocked the weapon and unloaded a single bullet, which he then left in the mailbox. He went to open the door and found it was unlocked. In his deranged mind, that meant he was welcome.

It was perfect.

He swung the door open and came face-to-face with 22-year-old Teresa Wallin. She had spent the day cleaning and running errands and been right in the middle of taking out the kitchen's garbage. She was headed to the front door when it suddenly swung open. It was a man, and he was armed.

Richard closed the door behind him and aimed his gun at her. The victim dropped her bag and lifted her hands in obvious shock.

Richard fired twice. The first bullet shot through the palm of her right hand, tore through her forearm, and exploded out of her elbow, hitting her in the head. The other tore through her cheek and broke her jawbone.

Teresa fell to the floor. Richard approached her and got down on his knees. He fired a third time, this time at close range into her brain, finally ending her short life.

Once he was certain she was dead, Richard grabbed her by the shoulders and dragged her corpse to one of the house's three bedrooms. Her gaping wounds were leaving a thick trail of blood across the floor. If he was not careful, she would lose more, and that would have been wasteful.

He needed a way to keep as much of the precious blood as possible. Looking around the house, he found a large spoon. From the pile of garbage Teresa dropped, he dug out an empty yogurt cup.

It was time for the Dracula killer to live up to the name.

Teresa's husband, David Wallin, would not be home for a while. A delivery driver for a linen company, he tended to work long hours, usually starting early in the morning. Today, he would be busy even longer because he was assigned to train Jim Cody, a new driver, and there was a problem out on the road to Lake Tahoe.

While Richard stalked the outside of the Wallin home, David and his trainee, Jim, loaded the truck and got ready for the drive across the Sierra Nevada. The truck began to break down shortly after they had gotten onto the interstate, leaving them with no choice but to pull in to a service station that was just down the road from his house. While David waited for the mechanic to repair the truck, his wife's lifeless body was being mutilated a block away.

With the truck seemingly up and running again, David and the trainee got back on the road to their destination. Unfortunately, their truck would break down a second time after they had started to drive up the mountains. They used a payphone to call a mechanic who arrived only to tell them that the truck would never make it all the way to Tahoe in its condition. The best idea was to head back, their truck still fully loaded with its cargo.

It had been a brutal waste of a day, David thought as he headed to the Slick Willies Bar after work. Long and unpleasant. He and Jim shared two pitchers of beer before David decided to head on home. He could never have imagined how much worse it was about to get. Not even in his worst nightmares.

The first sign that something was wrong was the darkness that permeated the house. Teresa liked to keep busy. Why would the lights be off, but the stereo left on?

Beyond the darkness, their pet German Shepherd, Brutus, sat waiting. The dog was restless and nervous. Something had happened here. David could tell that much when he flipped the switch and saw garbage all over the living room floor.

But why were there dark oil spots all over the rug? And why did they stretch in a trail leading to the bedroom he shared with his wife?

David was confused. He had to get to the bottom of this. He called out for Teresa but got no response.

He headed for the master bedroom and opened the door, and that's when he found her.

Teresa was almost completely naked, her legs splayed apart, exposing her vagina. The thick, bloody cord of her internal organs sat upon her open abdomen. Worst of all was her face.

His wife had suffered a horrific death. The last thing she felt was fear. He could see it on her face, still frozen with terror. Her eyes, once so warm and lovely, were still open wide.

David Wallin gave out a wail so loud that the entire neighborhood could feel the grief in the air.

Somehow, he managed to compose himself long enough to call his father and brother, John. When he hung up, he knew he could not stay in the house, so close to the lifeless body of his poor wife. He ran out the door and towards the neighbor's yard, hysterical and crying out, "My wife is dead!" It was his next-door neighbors who, in between their futile efforts to comfort the terrified man, made the call to the police.

David spotted his father's car parked outside. He panicked, realizing he had not told his family he would be leaving the house. He rushed out the door, hoping to make it to his own house before his parents did and spare them the horror of seeing Teresa.

But it was too late. He went inside and saw his mother and father in the kitchen, both of them shaken. They already saw her. The three of them remained there, mourning, while police came to the crime scene.

Even the most hardened and experienced among them would never forget what they were about to see.

XIV

The Hunt Begins

POLICE AND MEDIA DESCENDED UPON THE SCENE on Tioga Way later that evening. The street was quickly closed off, and yellow police tape was hung around the perimeter of the Wallin home. In order to best preserve all the evidence at the crime scene, the press and civilians alike were ordered to stay off the street.

Deputies made sure that the names of everyone who entered and left the house were written down. They could not take any chances with the integrity of a scene this horrific.

By then, Teresa's heartbroken parents had arrived. Leona and John Lahann could only stand to stay a short while before they drove away in tears. Detectives, at a loss for words in the face of this tragedy, could only promise to keep them updated.

Frank Davidson, part of the CSI, was the first one to find Richard's bullet within the mailbox. It was a .22-caliber bullet, something Lieutenant Ray Biondi and his team noticed right away. The same type of bullet had been used to kill Ambrose Griffin.

Had the same killer gone from distant, drive-by shootings to this sort of sadism in just a few weeks?

The garbage was still all over the living room floor. Among the debris were two brass shell casings, likely from the same gun.

The music coming from the stereo gave the room an even eerier feeling.

It was time for the hardest part: seeing the body for the first time.

Teresa Wallin lay stiff on the floor. Her sweater had been pulled up to expose her breasts, and her pants and underwear were around her ankles. The look on her face was disquieting. Her eyes were open wide, and her tongue had been pulled out of her mouth. Briefly, the detectives wondered if she had been raped or if this undressing was a way to further humiliate the victim. Only time—and testing—could tell.

She still wore all her jewelry. The valuables in the house had remained untouched. Money from the check Teresa had cashed that morning was still inside her purse. The thought that this could have been a financially-motivated crime seemed more and more unlikely.

Her abdominal cavity was nearly empty. Her organs were pulled out, some sitting on top of her, some falling to her side. A closer look revealed that one of her nipples had been sliced off. The killer had cut her from her sternum down to her hip, and had done so with so much force that both her sternum and her breast plate were hacked wide open.

Teresa's autopsy found a number of even more disturbing details. Though criminalist Alan Gilmore had tested the body for signs that she had been raped and found no evidence, the position of the organs suggested that the killer had "explored" or "played with" her insides. The knife had been thrust so deeply into her abdomen that it hit the base of the spinal column. The intestines had not been damaged, but the membrane and tissue connecting them had been severed, likely to get the organs out.

The spleen had been completely cut out of her body and was lying on her. Her stomach and liver had been cut with the knife. Hacking at the membrane connecting the intestines gave the killer access to Teresa's kidneys; one of them was nearly cut in two, while the other had been torn out and placed inside her chest. Her heart and diaphragm were punctured, and the lower portion of one of her lungs had been sawed off.

Most heartbreaking of all was the discovery of the three-month-old fetus still inside her womb.

Many of the officers present at the scene had never seen anything so gruesome in their lives. The image of the young lady's mutilated corpse would stay fresh in their minds for weeks. Even the most experienced among them had difficulty keeping their composure.

Ray Biondi took down notes while the CSI team took photographs of the scene. On the ground was a pencil, a book of matches, a blood-stained yogurt cup, and something else they could not quite make sense of at first. There were several bloodstains on the wooden floor around the body in the shape of little rings. Despite all the blood, there didn't seem to be any fingerprints, and the investigators determined that the killer had worn rubber gloves and cleaned up after himself.

The investigation stretched on late into the night and continued to the next morning. As was usual when someone is murdered, especially in such a violent way, the spouse was interviewed by police. Still, detectives had a hard time believing that poor David Wallin had been involved. Not only was he completely devastated, but he had a solid alibi.

Out in the yard, Sergeant Don Habecker found what he believed was the killer's escape route. A part of the yard was underwater, and a wooden board was set down like a small bridge toward the fence. Shoe prints, like those found in the house, were visible on the wood but became much harder to track down the path that led to the parking lot of the Town and Country Village Shopping Center. It would have been easy for the killer to slip by, unseen by neighbors, if he headed down this way.

However, a few people did claim to have seen a suspicious person on the day of the murder. Each gave a similar description: a dirty, skinny, weird white man in a bright orange parka. Another neighbor, this time a mother, came forward and told police that her five-year-old daughter had seen a large knife in a nearby storm drain.

It was bagged up and sent to the crime lab with the rest of the evidence, but was eventually found not to have been the murder weapon. The actual weapon, it was later discovered, had been left inside the home all along, placed beneath other dishes in the dish rack.

There was not much evidence, but what little they had was painting a picture of a very deranged killer.

XV

The Eve of the Massacre

LIKE AMBROSE GRIFFIN AND DOROTHY POLENSKE before her, Teresa Lynn Wallin had been a well-liked person. She was regarded as a pretty, sweet woman. Her best features were her bright blue eyes and her warm smile. She was a cheerful person who her friends remembered fondly for years. She seemed to radiate happiness.

Though they had not been married for long, she and her husband David had a happy and stable relationship. While she had recently been hired at a new job working for the state, she still managed to maintain a spotless home. The house had three bedrooms, and it was clear that she and David had made plans for children to occupy them in the future.

But that dream was dead because Teresa was dead, her bright soul brutally snuffed out before it could truly shine.

What reason would anyone have to kill a person like her?

Though the random, thrill-killer theory was still on the table, the Sacramento homicide detectives still had to look at the case from all possible angles. An attack this vicious could have been a crime of passion. Could Teresa have been murdered by somebody that she knew? Somebody other than her husband?

One unusual lead came when detectives went to interview David's two sisters. They were certain that Teresa had been murdered by a jealous woman that David had once dated. Ray Biondi would later identify this woman as Joyce Summers, though her real name was not given out.

Joyce was an obsessive woman. When she learned that David and Teresa were going to get married, she was devastated but undeterred. So intent she was on winning her old boyfriend back, she showed up at the wedding. She had followed David the entire time, repeatedly declaring her love for him. One of the sisters added that Joyce also claimed to have been part of a Satanic cult, and had psychic powers that allowed her to look into the future.

Police had not seriously considered the possibility that their suspect could have been a woman before this, but they knew they had to look at the case from all angles, no matter how far-fetched they might have seemed. The team sought out Joyce Summers and asked her where she had been on the 23rd of January.

But Joyce had a solid alibi. It was impossible for her to have done it.

Tensions continued to rise the longer Teresa's and Ambrose's cases went unsolved. The month of January saw an unusually high number of homicides that year. The East Area Rapist, who would remain unidentified and at large until 2018, had committed his 28th rape the month prior. It seemed that violence was becoming worryingly common.

Meanwhile, Richard Chase spent much of his time at home either watching television or waiting on newspapers detailing his crimes. While police searched for their killer, Richard was seen exploring a different neighborhood. The day after he murdered Teresa, he was spotted on Park Estates Drive. His orange parka and disheveled appearance made him stick out. At 11 in the morning, a couple noticed him looking around a neighbor's property. When Richard noticed a sign warning of a guard dog, he left.

A little over an hour later, he knocked at a woman's door and asked if she had any old magazines he could have. She replied she did not, and Richard seemed to reject this answer. He tried to ask her again, but the woman quickly retreated inside, shutting the door in his face.

Richard spent much of the day knocking at different houses and asking for magazines. He preferred popular publications like *Mad* and *Cosmopolitan* but would take whatever the residents would give him. Most of them, however, just hoped this dirty stranger would leave them alone. Richard, on the other hand, only wanted to read the articles he hoped had been written about his crimes.

The following day, the team of detectives interviewed Daniel Owens and his wife, who sold Richard the pair of Labrador puppies a few months earlier. The couple recalled the details of the transaction and later recalled a more disturbing memory: the day after Richard bought the two puppies, the Owens went to their back patio and discovered one of the dogs they had kept from the litter dead.

It had not died a natural death. It had been shot in the head and its belly was ripped open. Its organs, including the kidneys, were pulled out of its body. He had drunk some of its blood. When they sent the dog for an autopsy, they learned that the animal had not only been tortured before it was killed, but the killer had taken some of its organs.

Then there was a familiar finding. Fragments of .22-caliber bullets were embedded in the dead creature's flesh.

That evening, Richard spoke to his mother over the phone. Beatrice listened as her son spoke on and on about UFOs, rockets, and "little green men." According to her, Richard had sounded quite happy.

XVI

Like Something Out of a Nightmare

THIRTY-SIX-YEAR-OLD EVELYN MIROTH WAS A popular woman. She had many friends and relatives in the neighborhood and often babysat for them. Though she was the divorced single mother to two boys, 13-year-old Vernon and 6-year-old Jason, she still managed to lead an active social life and even had a new steady boyfriend. Her home was right across the street to one of her best friends, Neone Grangaard. The two women bonded over their young children.

On Friday, January 27, Neone had a day off from her job at the post office and wanted to take a fun trip. It was still snowing at the Sierra Nevada mountains, and she thought an afternoon playing in the snow with her children would be a fine way to spend the day. She also wanted to invite Evelyn along, but her friend was busy babysitting her nephew. She did ask, however, if Jason could go instead.

The women were excited as they prepared for the outing. Evelyn still needed to rent a pair of snowshoes for her son from a nearby sporting goods store, and this delayed Neone's plan to leave by nine that morning, though Neone did not mind and instead arranged for them to leave by ten.

As Neone waited, she noticed a red station wagon pull into Evelyn's driveway. The vehicle, which belonged to an older friend of Evelyn named Danny Meredith, was a common sight in the neighborhood. The car pulled away but was back before ten thirty in the morning, after Danny had picked up the snowshoes for Jason.

Neone was certain that her friend would send Jason over soon. When another half hour passed without Jason appearing at her doorstep, Neone had begun to get worried and a little annoyed. Evelyn was always a responsible woman. It was unlike her to be so late.

She sent Tracy, her six-year-old daughter, across the street, to see what was taking Jason so long. The little girl knocked and got no response. It appeared that nobody was home. However, when she peered through the window, she swore she saw somebody moving around inside.

Why wouldn't they answer the door if they were home, Neone wondered.

This was indeed very strange for Evelyn. To double-check, Neone took her daughter by the hand and headed to Evelyn's house. By now, Danny's red station wagon was gone. More evidence that Evelyn had left without a word, though Catherine Belli, who lived right next door to Evelyn, never saw anybody leave the house.

With their trip now delayed over an hour, Neone became restless. She considered leaving without Jason. But she still could not shake the vague feeling that something was very wrong.

Neone returned to her own home and was just about to drive off when she noticed Nancy Turner, a mutual friend and neighbor to both women, arrive home from a shopping trip. When Neone explained what had happened, Nancy began to worry as well. After leaving her items at home, Nancy went to the back door of the Miroth house.

The door was unlocked.

She went inside and looked around. A little deeper inside, Nancy came across a horrific sight. The bloodied corpse of 50-year-old Danny Meredith lay face down on the floor.

Disbelief, then terror ran through Nancy's mind. A terrified shriek erupted from her lungs as she ran back out to Neone. "Something's wrong!" she cried. "He's on the floor, and there's blood all over the place. Call for help!"

The news traveled fast on Merrywood Drive. When two movers with the Salvation Army who had been assisting a neighbor heard about the shocking sight, they alerted the Sheriff's Department through the switchboard on their radio-equipped truck. While they waited for the police to arrive, the men decided to go inside the Miroth home to see if they could help what they assumed was merely an injured person. When they got there, they looked through the living room window and saw the man lying motionless on the floor. Bloodstains surrounded his body. They realized there was nothing two movers could do for this man.

Sheriff's Deputy Ivan Clark arrived at the scene just after noon. The officer headed for the house and saw the crowd of neighbors gathered outside the Miroth house. It was a bit excessive for such a routine call, he thought briefly, but he was used to dealing with nosy neighbors whenever he showed up at a scene.

Sheriff Clark, who had assumed that Danny Meredith had simply passed out drunk on Evelyn's rug, went inside the house through the back door. In the hallway, he found Danny. He had lost so much blood that the stains around him looked nearly black.

He looked closer at the body. There were two bullet wounds to Danny's head. Someone had shot him. Murdered him.

So what happened to the woman of the house and her boy? Thankfully, 13-year-old Vernon was at school, but Jason?

He found a trail of blood that led to the bathroom. Like the rug in the hall, the bathroom floor was covered with dark red stains. The tub was full of bloody water, as though someone had been badly hurt while they were in the middle of bathing.

Alarm bells went off in the officer's mind. He went back out to the hallway and noticed the trail leading to the master bedroom. Cautiously, he approached the room and peered inside.

And there Evelyn was. Like Teresa Wallin, she was undressed. Her legs were left wide open. She had been eviscerated from her sternum down to the hip. Her organs had been pulled out of her abdominal cavity, defiled by some madman's curiosity. There even were ringlet-like stains on the carpet around her.

Ivan Clark composed himself. Then all he could think about were those awful photographs of Teresa Wallin's mutilated corpse. Someone had done the exact same thing to Evelyn. The killer struck again not only once, but twice in one day.

Ivan sealed off the area with police tape while the others arrived. He stood in front of the main door, making sure nobody could go in and tamper with the crime scene. When the other police arrived, they saw Ivan looking pale and afraid. Instantly they knew that whatever was in there had to be horrific.

Ray Biondi and his team began to look around the house. The gate leading to the back yard was unlocked, and the patio door had been left open, though there was also the possibility the killer had entered through the garage, which had been left unlocked after Evelyn finished mowing the lawn that day. They found bloodstains and a cigarette butt on the ground, which they collected.

The house was dead silent. The officers moved around the house, past Danny's corpse, and noticed that many things had been disturbed. The phone had been knocked off the hook. There was blood inside a drawer in the kitchen.

In the living room, they found .22-caliber bullets on the floor.

This killer was a savage one.

Next, they went to look at Evelyn's body. Like Teresa Wallin, the mother of two had been left in a humiliating pose. A realization struck them. Both Teresa and Evelyn had been mutilated, but Danny was still fully dressed, his body intact aside from the gaping wounds caused by being shot in the head at close range. The autopsy later revealed that, unlike Teresa, Evelyn had been sexually assaulted. The killer's semen was found within her rectum. She had been anally raped with one of the two butcher knives that they found beside her with such force that the inside of the buttocks had been cut open. There were two cuts to her rectal wall, and her uterus had been severed in six different parts.

The trauma to her body had been extensive. Alongside her genital wounds, investigators found that her abdomen had been cut open with a cross-shaped incision. The liver had been cut and, also like with Teresa Wallin, the membranes connecting her organs had been severed; a large portion of her intestines was outside of the body, as was her stomach.

Postmortem wounds included eight superficial cuts to her neck and one along the inner corner of her eyelid, which had been inverted. Evelyn's right eye had been pulled out of her socket and was dangling on the side of her face.

The killer seemed to only butcher women. Had these crimes been sexually motivated? Or were they dealing with a violent misogynist whose hatred was growing with each kill?

And what happened to the young boy in the house?

XVII

A New Search Begins

THEY HAD BEEN SO OVERWHELMED BY THE state of Evelyn's body that they nearly overlooked the other small figure lying on the bed. Jason Miroth, all dressed up and ready for a trip to the mountains, lay dead not far from his mother. He had also been shot with a .22-caliber bullet.

The officers were used to dealing with dead adults, but the sight of an innocent, dead child was almost too much to bear. Still, the investigation had to continue.

Outside, they tried to put the evidence they had together. A footprint in the soil matching the ones found at the Wallin home was found outside the Miroth house. Everyone checked the soles of their shoes, and it was determined that the prints were left by a man's tennis shoes. No one at the scene was wearing something like that. Next, they tried talking to the neighbors. Although nobody had seen anyone leave the house after Danny Meredith had arrived, the officers hoped that maybe someone noticed a suspicious person before that.

An 11-year-old girl gave a familiar description. That day she had seen a skinny, brown-haired, white male in his early 20s. He had been wearing a brightly colored jacket.

They also realized that Danny's red station wagon was not in the driveway. Had the killer stolen his vehicle? The detectives made sure to put out a detailed alert about the missing car.

While the police had been investigating the house, the Miroths' phone kept ringing. Deep into the afternoon, a frantic woman arrived, with her husband Tony coming by about an hour later. Her name was Karen Ferreria, and she was looking for her son, 22-month-old David. They had been informed earlier of what happened inside the house.

The police realized with horror that there had been another child involved this entire time.

And he was not in the house. In fact, there was no sign of little David Ferreria.

With renewed urgency, the police searched the house again, and Detective Homen made a terrifying discovery. There was a .22-caliber bullet hole in a bloody pillow within the crib in one of the bedrooms. Scattered on the floor were his various belongings as well as bloody footprints. Some of the gore in the blood-filled tub was later determined to be some of the baby's brain matter, spilled when the killer hacked open the back of his skull.

But where was the baby now?

Again, the police were getting desperate. If there was even the slightest chance that David Ferreria was still alive, then they did not have a second to lose. But how were they supposed to go forward with no real suspects?

Though the description of the possible killer was consistent across witnesses, there was nothing particularly distinguishing about the details they had given. There were many skinny, unkempt, young white men in the area. They could not possibly check them all out. At one point, even members of the Charles Manson family had been considered.

There was a hopeful turn after the officers sent out a bulletin to the press, summarizing the gruesome events of the macabre murder. A nearby detective, Mike Hash, who had seen a police sketch of the intruder at the Edwards' home, saw a man who he thought looked eerily similar. This stringy-haired, thin man was even wearing a bright green parka.

The man was soon identified as 23-year-old Keith Roberts, a laborer for a local construction company. He had been visiting his mother at the Sandpiper Apartments when the presence of the police piqued his curiosity. That was when Mike Hash, who had been searching the area, spotted him.

Interestingly, Keith had been a former classmate of Teresa Wallin, whom he had known as Teresa Lahann when they were at Encina High School together a few years back. When the police searched through his belongings, they found an orange windbreaker and a pair of Adidas tennis shoes.

As convincing as Mike Hash initially was of Keith's guilt, the other detectives soon realized that Keith could not have been their suspect. The print left by his shoes did not match the ones left at the crime scene. He also had been working while the crimes had been committed.

The police went on to interview a number of local eccentrics, including a mentally ill man and another who carried a bejeweled, ceremonial dagger. However, none of them were the suspect. It looked like they were back to square one.

It was time to lay out everything they had. Lieutenant Ray Biondi, who had received some special psychological training by the FBI, helped make a psychological profile of the killer.

By now, everyone was certain that the suspect was a young white man who neglected both hygiene and grooming. He likely suffered a severe mental illness, which they determined not only due to the severity of the crimes but also due to the fact that they had all been carried out in broad daylight. He left behind footprints and cigarette butts that could be used to tie him to the murders and even left the knives out in the open. Unlike most killers, he seemed to do very little to conceal what he had done.

This man was probably a sexually frustrated and incompetent loner without a stable job or close, meaningful relationships. The crimes he had committed, as horrific as they were, were not sophisticated ones.

It was the profile of what came to be known as a disorganized killer. It is still used by law enforcement and the FBI to this day.

More tips from alleged witnesses continued to roll in. One man claimed that he saw a man matching Richard's description driving some sort of old pickup truck with an out-of-state license plate. The driver had been headed down the road when he suddenly stepped out of the vehicle and started walking around in a traffic lane outside a Wells Fargo, holding up a line of cars that had been behind him.

On January 28, 71-year-old Retta Scott called to report an incident where she nearly collided with an erratic, long-haired man driving a red station wagon while she was leaving a department store. That had taken place at the intersection of El Camino and Merrywood Drive, Evelyn Miroth's neighborhood.

Eventually, police came across the Big Five Sporting Goods store where Richard had purchased his gun. California law required that anyone purchasing a firearm had to sign documents and give their license plate number, which Richard had done when he lied about never having been a mental health patient.

However, the fact that Richard had made this purchase around Christmas muddied the trail considerably. Not only that, but a .22-caliber handgun was an incredibly common weapon.

They were starting to make progress, but the most important question remained unanswered: What had the killer done with little David Ferreria, and where was the body now?

XVIII

Finally Closing In

DANNY MEREDITH'S CAR WAS EVENTUALLY found abandoned within the area of the Sandpiper Apartments Complex, some distance away from both the Wallin and Miroth neighborhoods.

Another breakthrough in the case came on the morning of January 28, when two detectives, Bill Roberts and Carol Daly, who had been assigned to look into the backgrounds of Richard's victims, got a call from the retired county marshal. He told them about an incident that involved a creepy man and his daughter-in-law, Nancy Holden.

She had decided to report the sighting at his urgency after she noticed that Richard bore a strong resemblance to the police sketch of the Edwards' burglar.

On the morning Teresa Wallin had been murdered, Nancy had had an uncomfortable reunion with her old classmate Richard Chase at a grocery store that Teresa had been known to shop at. At first, the tip did not seem very helpful, but when the detectives ran his information through the DMV's computer, they found that this Richard Trenton Chase did at least match the physical description of the killer. The last address on file was apartment number 12 at the Watt Avenue Complex.

The two detectives tried to pay Richard a visit, but instead, they were met by a man named Gerald Berringer. Gerald, who had only been living in apartment number 12 for about two weeks, had never met Richard. Discouraged, the detectives left, unaware that their killer was only three doors down the hall in apartment number 15.

Wayne Irey, an officer assigned to the task force for the East Area Rapist, still had an interest in Nancy Holden's story. He called her later the same day and asked her more about the incident. When she said that Richard wore blue jeans, black tennis shoes, and most importantly, a bright orange parka, Officer Irey began to suspect that they had their man.

Detective Bill Roberts later searched through police records for anything that mentioned Richard Chase. He found that Richard had had a number of arrests from the late 1960s and early 1970s. Most of them were charges for drug possession, but in 1968, he had been arrested as a suspect in a shooting. In 1973, Richard had faced a concealed weapons charge. Three years later, he was arrested after he escaped from the psychiatric ward at the American River Hospital.

It was Richard's latest arrest that helped break the case. In 1977, after he had been arrested at Pyramid Lake, Richard's information revealed that he had moved into apartment number 15 at the same complex as before.

Officer Irey got the feeling they were at last closing in on their killer. He took a closer look at Richard's old mug shots and compared them to the police sketch of the burglar on Burnece Street. The resemblance was uncanny, to say the least. Then he decided to draw the mustache and goatee that Richard had on his mugshot onto the sketch. He even showed his handiwork to one of the women working at the records counter, and she believed the similarities were remarkable.

He could hardly believe it. There was almost no way this was not their man. Even though some of the other officers were not as convinced of Irey's findings, he was sure of it. Enthusiastic, even. Irey called the DMV's law enforcement department and ordered more information on Richard Chase, including recent photographs and fingerprints.

The place of residence was listed as 2934 Watt Avenue. Apartment number 15.

Irey hurried to Ray Biondi's office and gave him all the information he had gathered, including Nancy Holden's story. Though initially doubtful, Biondi became curious, and soon seriously considered the possibility that this was their man. It was too good a lead not to follow up on.

It looked like it was time to pay a visit to Richard Trenton Chase. After all, they needed to cover all their bases.

XIX

The Vampire's Capture

ON THE EVENING OF THE DAY THAT NANCY
Holden gave her witness statement, Officer Wayne Irey
went down to the Watt Avenue Apartment Complex in an
unmarked car. With him was Bill Roberts, and Ken Baker, a new
detective who thought the entire trip would be a waste of time. As
they pulled up, one of them saw the possible suspect's vehicle listed
in their reports: an old, brown pickup truck.

At nearly six, they went upstairs and came to the apartment
manager's office. They met the landlord, a woman named Betty
Tietjen. She confirmed that Richard Chase was indeed a tenant at

the complex and had been for a while. He lived on the ground floor, in apartment number 15. She agreed to go downstairs with them.

They asked Betty what she could tell them about Richard. She recalled that he was an odd, quiet young man who liked to keep to himself. Other than his mother Beatrice, who paid his rent and dropped off groceries for him every month, he hardly ever had any visitors. He did not even seem to have any friends. In fact, he only spoke to his mother through a crack in the door when she came to drop off groceries.

The woman brought up a comment that Beatrice had made about her son's drug use, referring to him as a "victim of LSD abuse." She and Richard were not on good terms, and the two of them were currently refusing to see each other face-to-face.

It was clear that Richard was a difficult person at times, but Betty had never seen him do anything outrageous or illegal. The worst she could recall was when he had walked around the complex openly carrying a rifle. The neighbors were troubled by this, but there were no laws forbidding him from owning the weapon, nor was he breaking any of the building's rules by keeping it with him. When she asked him to conceal the weapon with a blanket, he readily did as he was told.

Richard could be a nuisance, sure. But was he a murderer? That was something the detectives could only learn by talking to the man himself.

They asked Betty to show them the parking lot. There, they found Richard's pickup truck again, a 1966 Ford Ranchero with a Florida license plate.

Anxiety crept up on the men. It seemed as though everything was falling in to place much faster than they had anticipated. The most critical part, however, was yet to come.

They walked to the north side of the building until they came upon apartment number 15. "Sheriff's Department," Bill Roberts called out as he knocked on the door. "We just want to talk to you, Richard."

Each of them tried to coax Richard out, careful that the man might charge out of the apartment armed, but no response came from beyond the door. Was he even in there? Betty had warned them that he was reclusive.

Without a search warrant, they could not get Betty to unlock the door for them to check. Instead, she gave them a key to the empty apartment next to his. Detective Ken Baker went in alone and pressed his ear against the thin walls. He could hear the sound of someone moving within Richard's apartment. Richard lived alone, so this had to be him.

Next, Detective Roberts decided to give Richard a phone call. The phone rang twice before they heard Richard's high-pitched, eerie voice on the other end. "Hello?" he asked.

"Richard?" asked Bill Roberts.

"Yes," Richard said. "Do I know you?"

"Bill, remember? We met once a while back."

Richard did not say anything else. He hung up the phone and did not answer when they tried calling again. But they did not need to. Now they knew their suspect was inside.

They called Biondi for guidance, and Biondi told them he was sending more officers, including detectives, to their location.

All they needed now was to figure out a way to get him out. It sounded relatively easily, but there was a good chance they could mess things up if they were not careful enough. Further guidance from Biondi gave them more ideas, and the plan they ultimately came up with was a simple one. They were going to trick and trap him.

Outside his door, the men loudly discussed giving up and heading home. Wayne Irey went down one end of the hall, and Ken Baker went down the other.

A few minutes later, the door finally opened. Richard emerged carrying a McDonald's box. He started to head in the direction of his car when Officer Irey jumped out at him.

Panicked, Richard hurried down the opposite way, only to find his path blocked by Detective Baker. Eyes wide with shock, Richard tried to throw the box at Baker and slip by him to make a run for it, but Baker deflected the box with his gun.

Richard was not agile enough to avoid the blow that was about to come to his head.

Ken Baker stood before the collapsed man, his .45-caliber handgun in his grip. He kept his eyes on the suspect, who got back up to his feet quicker than he had anticipated. Luckily, Irey was not far behind. The officer came running and tackled Richard, holding his writhing body tight.

Though he had been caught, Richard was not going down without a fight. Even as Irey twisted the barrel of his .38-caliber pistol to the side of his head, Richard tried hard to break free from the officer's grasp. The skinny man was stronger than he looked, and the muscular Wayne Irey was struggling to keep Richard from slipping away.

The truth was, Officer Irey did not want to shoot. Though he had been silently planning to kill Richard if they found David Ferreria's body inside the apartment, he knew he could not do it. He did not have it in him to go through with killing a person. That was what separated him from murderers like Richard Chase.

He dropped his own weapon and focused on disarming the suspect.

Meanwhile, Baker was trying to put Richard in handcuffs. It was difficult, even between him and Irey. He managed to cuff one wrist and tried for the other. Without the use of an arm, Richard could not keep up the fight to hold on to the gun under his arm. Officer Irey yanked it away, and at last, Baker cuffed Richard's other wrist. It was over for him.

Bill Roberts, who had been on the phone with Biondi during the fray, ran toward his partners after Betty screamed that his partners needed help. Biondi arrived soon after. Irey was eager to show him the contents of the tan-colored wallet that he found in one of Richard's pockets. Inside was a driver's license, but it was not Richard's.

It belonged to Danny Meredith.

Also inside were various cards as well as pictures of Evelyn and Jason Miroth. Inside the McDonald's box that Richard threw at Baker was a pair of bloodied rubber gloves and rags, .22-caliber bullets, a key ring with 16 keys, David Ferreria's diaper pin, and an envelope with brain matter sealed inside.

This was it. They had finally caught the killer. Now only one piece of the puzzle was left. Where was David Ferreria?

In the back of the patrol car, Richard ignored all their questions. Instead, he muttered to himself, saying, "I haven't done anything. All I did in my apartment was kill a few dogs."

XX

The Interrogation Room

WHEN IT WAS TIME FOR THE INTERVIEW THAT evening, Richard seemed to have calmed down considerably. At the station, he was told to sit in an interrogation room alongside Officer Irey and Detective Roberts.

The men, not wanting to risk any possible legal errors, made sure to hand Richard a card that listed his rights. Once they were certain Richard Chase understood the situation, they began their questions.

Had he killed the woman who lived on Tiago Way, Teresa Wallin? Richard denied it.

Had he ever killed anyone before? Richard denied this too.

Officer Irey informed Richard that the crime lab would be testing all the stains on his clothing to see if they matched any possible victims. Upon hearing this, Richard began to panic again. He asked to keep his empty gun holster as it comforted him, but this request was denied. His eyes flooded with tears, but he held them back. "My apartment's a lot cleaner, huh?"

His response was nonsensical, but it seemed to take the edge off his anxiety.

Had Richard been in the area of the Country Club Centre lately, they asked. Richard said no. He claimed he had not bothered anyone.

"You ran away from us," Irey pointed out. "Why?"

Richard said he had been half asleep when he had come out of his apartment. He said all that had been inside the box was paper. He denied ever having been in the area of any of the murders and even denied having met Nancy Holden.

They asked where the blood came from, and Richard said it came from dogs. They asked if he killed them, and Richard replied that he had. This he said with some reluctance, almost like he was starting to feel guilt. He would not talk about anything else but the dogs. Richard admitted he had killed dogs, several of them. But he was adamant that he had never seen David Ferreria.

Detectives Don Habecker and Fred Homen went to Richard's apartment while the interview was going on. They found no sign of David, but there were several other things that caught their attention.

The entire place stank of rot and decay, no doubt due in part to the blood that stained nearly every inch of the place. It was all over the bedroom, the bathroom, and even a big puddle in the kitchen. A bloodstained loaf of French bread sat on the couch. The unwashed dishes they found around the apartment contained blood, as did a cup in the bathroom's medicine cabinet, and the putrid-smelling blender in the kitchen. The stuff was on every surface the two men could imagine.

Among the blood were .22-caliber bullets and bone fragments. They could not yet tell what they were from. Other weapons found in the apartment included a blood-drenched hatchet and machete.

There were bullet holes in the walls and hair in strange places: in the soap and in a little bag in the medicine cabinet. Inside the freezer, they found a half-gallon container filled with the meat, kidneys, liver, and heart of an unidentified animal.

Richard lived in appalling conditions besides the blood; there were feces all over the floor of the bedroom.

There were piles of newspapers. Upon closer inspection, they saw that articles about recent murders and ads for free dogs had been circled. On the walls were diagrams of human anatomy that had likely been taken from the various medical books Richard had collected. He also had reading materials on subjects such as totalitarianism, psychics, guns, and the Old West.

Inside a spiral notebook where crude sketches of guns and swastikas, as well as the phrase, *My name is Richard Chase. I am a 01000 computer. I was sent here from the year 10,000.*

And then there was the yearbook.

The detectives flipped it open. It was from Mira Loma High School. The class of 1966. They found Richard's picture among the sophomores. The boy smiled at them from within the pages. More than ten years had passed since that photo had been taken, and the now wild-eyed, deranged Richard bore almost no resemblance to his younger self. They could hardly believe this was the same person.

There were notes at the front and back of the yearbook, messages that served as a proof of a time when Richard was not a loner. People liked being around him once. He had friends then. Now this well-groomed boy was a killer stuck in an interrogation room.

Before the interview, the police took pictures of Richard for their records.

He continued to deny any involvement with the murders, but when the officers presented him with a photograph of little David Ferreria, he seemed to lose his composure for a moment. Still, he denied having killed anyone. This went on until Irey and Homen were replaced by Pat O'Neal and Tom Robinson, two more seasoned detectives. They were the first to accuse Richard of having drunk the blood of his victims.

Richard said the claims were ludicrous. He said he would never have gotten mixed up with something as deranged as cannibalism. He said he was being framed by Italians, and when asked what he thought about eating human flesh, Richard responded with, "The Nazis ate a lot."

The real suspect was some blond guy, Richard stated. Or someone that had kept coming in and out of his apartment.

Then, Richard only spoke about the dogs again. He said he killed an Irish setter by the Folsom Lake as well as the two Labrador puppies he had purchased from Daniel Owens.

The interrogators never got what they wanted out of Richard Chase during that long interview. They never got the chance because Richard was sent to jail, his clothing was sent for testing, and Farris Salamy, one of the top public defenders in the country, took him on as a client.

That same evening, when the officers were off for the night, the East Area Rapist struck again.

XXI

The Recovery

I T WAS IMMEDIATELY CLEAR THAT RICHARD CHASE
would not survive long in prison.

On his first night in the Sacramento County Jail, the other
inmates were in a frenzy. They knew about the newcomer and what
he had done, and they wanted him dead. Some of the men urinated
in cups, which they flung into Richard's cell. Some threw their
feces. Others promised the guards that they would kill him as soon
as they got the chance.

Richard had to be moved to a single, isolated cell.

He was soon visited by two doctors identified as Dr. True and Dr. Whipple. Richard spoke to them openly about high school and his youth, but was hesitant to give details about his psychiatric history. When they asked what was on his mind, Richard said he was thinking about "normal things." When they asked him to elaborate, he said, "an exploding 747 jetliner." He also talked about UFOs and the Italian mob that was after him. He also claimed to be Jewish, though this was untrue.

Richard was nervous about needles and having his blood drawn, as he still worried his supply was low, but he was eager to see a doctor, hoping that there would finally be a cure for his unexplained illness.

Meanwhile, the search for David Ferreria continued. Among those looking for him was Deputy William Schneider, who was particularly invested. For six weeks, every day of the week, he worked 18-hour shifts. While other officers began to distance themselves from the harrowing mystery, Schneider's resolve only strengthened.

It did not matter that the boy was almost certainly dead. He wanted this victim to be found, and on February 1st, 1978,

Schneider came to the Watt Avenue Apartment Complex with a bloodhound.

Karen Ferreria had provided him with some of David's clothing, giving the dog a scent to follow. The dog sniffed and led Schneider to the rear parking lot, close to the Sandpiper Apartments where Danny Meredith's car had been found. The deputy followed the dog until it came to the Del Paso Country Club golf course.

Nothing was found on the golf course itself, but there was a small, surprisingly deep lake close by. It took two days to drain the lake, but there was no sign of the David Ferreria at the bottom.

The month wore on, and spring was on its way. Grass and other plant life had begun to grow, and Schneider knew this would make it much more difficult for them to find more evidence. With little time to lose, he paid a visit to Beatrice Chase, who was hostile and denied Richard's involvement in any crime, despite all the evidence. Nothing was found on her property.

Maps found in Richard's apartment were too nonsensical for officers to follow, and Schneider's plan to disguise himself as an inmate and gain Richard's trust was deemed too risky to try. So desperate were they that they even spoke to a psychic who, while holding little David's clothing, claimed to have visions of him somewhere where there were "lots of picnic tables."

Finally, there seemed to be a break. From within the Sacramento County Jail, an inmate named Wes Garrison had gotten Richard to talk about his crimes. According to Garrison, Richard said he murdered people because he needed blood and was tired of hunting animals for it. He said he drank the baby's blood and then threw it in the garbage.

Chasing this lead, they decided to search through the city's garbage again despite having already done so during the initial investigation. They had not gotten far when a citizen called to report "body parts" that he had found on the bank of a nearby creek.

They turned out to be deer bones.

David Ferreria was finally found in late March somewhere rather unexpected.

Oscar Rossow, a janitor for the Arcade Wesleyan Church, was making his usual rounds when he noticed something odd. The gate behind the church was unlocked, and not too far in the distance was a cardboard box.

Oscar thought little of it until the smell hit him. It was the pungent, faintly sweet smell of something that had been dead for a while. He wondered if somebody had dumped a deceased pet behind the building. But it was not an animal, he soon realized. It was a dead child.

The pastor of the church, though visibly shaken by what the janitor had told him, made the call to police. Within no time, Lieutenant Biondi and his team were at the scene.

David Ferreria, who was still wearing Sesame Street trousers, had been decapitated. His blond head was hidden beneath his own torso. Alongside the corpse were the keys to Danny Meredith's red station wagon.

Police arrived and covered the area to shield the crime scene from the press. Then they inspected the body and found that the baby had been shot on the right side of the head and stabbed in the back of the skull, creating holes that Richard used to gain access to the brain. The scrotum had been slashed, and seven of the boy's ribs had been broken.

The police had known there was no hope that David could be found alive, but they never expected to see something like this.

At the very least, the poor child's family would know for sure what happened and could mourn without any false hopes lingering in their minds.

XXII

The End of the Horror

DURING THE TRIAL, IT WAS DETERMINED THAT Richard Chase had used that little yogurt cup he found in Teresa Wallin's trash to collect the blood from the corpses. At first, he denied this. Then he said he had been set up by Italians that were out to get him. Then he said he had been set up by the neighbors who had been poisoning him for years with iodine and mercury, making him desperately sick. Then, he finally told the court what he really believed.

His heart was shrinking, and he did not want to die. In order to save his own life, he had to end the lives of others. It was not that he wanted to, but he was convinced that this was the only way. The only thing that could save him was the blood of other humans. He did not want to think about what he had done or remember it. He just wanted the pain to end.

But he had not stopped with just the blood. Richard had eaten parts of little David's brain before he dumped the body behind the Arcade Wesleyan Church. He said he could not remember doing any of this.

"I couldn't cope with the world anymore," Richard said during the trial. "Every time I tried to get up and act like a human being, I couldn't because of the weakness. Mental illness makes me get dizzy and lose my sense of reality. It puts me to sleep, kind of."

Anyone could tell that Richard was an unwell person, but was he truly insane? If this cannibal vampire wasn't crazy, then who was?

That June and up until the start of the trial in 1979, Ronald W. Tocherterman, the lead prosecutor on the case, studied the extensive history of blood-drinking rituals and cannibalism. It turned out that the practice, as macabre as it seemed, was a bigger part of human history than he had realized. He, along with two court-appointed prosecutors, studied Richard and eventually found him sane—and guilty.

Richard was a sick, sick man. But he knew right from wrong. He apologized for the murders. He said he was weak in heart as well as in mind.

On May 8, 1979, 29-year-old Richard Trenton Chase was found guilty of first-degree murder of Ambrose Griffin, Teresa Wallin, Evelyn Miroth, Daniel Meredith, Jason Miroth, and little David Ferreria. He was sentenced to death row at the San Quentin State Penitentiary, but never made it to his date with the gas chamber.

Richard's father wept. "Society will kill my son. I think I've known that from the start," he said to a reporter. "And maybe it's right; I don't know. There isn't a day that goes by that I don't think about the people he killed. I've cried a lot over the past year, and I don't know if it's been more for those people than for Rick."

On December 26, 1980, Richard was found dead in his cell by an overdose of hoarded antidepressant medication.

The horror was over. The Vampire of Sacramento had slain itself.

Conclusion

NOBODY COULD DENY THAT THE STORY OF THE Sacramento Vampire is a tragedy.

Richard Trenton Chase was a killer. He lacked empathy for others. He left his victims in positions that were so gruesome that they haunted law enforcement.

Richard Chase was a person who suffered every moment of his life.

Schizophrenia is a terrifying disease. Despite the leaps and bounds in research, modern medicine still has a limited understanding of why this terrible condition affects so many and how to best treat it. Even with care, the quality of life for so many schizophrenic patients is something nobody would ever envy.

It is difficult to imagine the fear and heartbreak that Richard Chase's parents felt when they learned that their only son had this mysterious illness nearly 50 years ago, or when they watched their son's condition deteriorate over the years—to say nothing about the horrific crimes he would go on to commit. There is no doubt that his parents loved and cared for him, but their denial of the severity of his issues only contributed to the tragedy of it all.

Was Richard Chase innately evil? In a way, the answer to that question doesn't really matter. What does matter is the fact that Richard could have been helped, but he wasn't. Because of this, six innocent people lost their lives at his hands. Not only had Richard been failed by the system, but so had his victims.

The yearbook he kept in apartment number 15 so many years after he left high school was proof of the possibility of another life. Who would Richard have been if it had not been for the defective condition of his own brain?

And who would his victims have become had they never crossed paths with Richard Trenton Chase, the Vampire of Sacramento?

References

"Richard Chase" Retrieved from https://murderpedia.org/male.C/c/chase-richard.htm

Biondi, R. Hecox, W. (2017) *A Thirst for Blood: The True Story of California's Vampire Killer* Open Road Media

Sullivan, K. (2012) *Vampire: The Richard Chase Murders* Wild Blue Press

"Chase, Richard - fall 2005" Retrieved from
http://maamodt.asp.radford.edu/Psyc%20405/serial%20killers/Chase,%20Richard%20-%20fall,%202005.pdf

Turner, J. "The Psychopathy of Richard Trenton Chase" Retrieved from
https://www.academia.edu/4302178/The_Psychopathology_of_Richard_Trenton_Chase

Davila, R. "Obituary: Veteran public defender Farris N. Salamy, 84, represented notorious killers" Retrieved from
https://www.sacbee.com/news/local/obituaries/article2590748.html

"Episode 245: Richard Chase Part 1 - The Cat Tree" Retrieved from
https://www.lastpodcastontheleft.com/episodes/2017/12/29/episode-245-richard-chase-part-i-the-cat-tree

"Episode 246: Richard Chase Part II - Mrs Dracul" Retrieved from
https://www.lastpodcastontheleft.com/episodes/2017/12/29/episode-246-richard-chase-part-ii-mrs-dracul

"'The Vampire of Sacramento' Pt 1: Richard Trenton Chase" Retrieved from
https://www.stitcher.com/podcast/parcast/serial-killers/e/64413583

"Richard Chase Arrest and Trial" Retrieved from
https://californiarevealed.org/islandora/object/cavpp%3A78316

Siino, A. "Our Morbid History" Retrieved from https://www.newsreview.com/sacramento/our-morbid-history/content?oid=25246046

Ramsland, K. "The Making of a Vampire" Retrieved from
https://web.archive.org/web/20071006064140/http://www.crimelibrary.com/serial_killers/weird/chase/index_1.html

"The Vampire Killer" Retrieved from
https://web.archive.org/web/20071011181140/http://robertkressler.com/ex_fights.htm

Acknowledgments

This is a special thanks to the following readers who have taken time out of their busy schedule to be part of the True Crime Seven Team. Thank you all so much for all the feedback and support!

James, Patricia Oliver, Rebecca Donnell, Jo Donna Hoevet, Tamara, Joan Baker, Jamie Bothen, Marty Fox, Dezirae, Christy Riemenschneider, Valencia, Tonja Marshall, Donna Reif, Marcie Walters, Kathy Morgan, Rebecca Stallman Catazaro, Anna McCown, Jason C. Tillery, Tina Shattuck, Lisa Marie Fraser, Penelope Bieniek, Lee Fowley, Courtney Waggoner, Sandy Van Domelen, Rebecca Ednie, Dallas Packer, Karen Harris, Paul Kelley, Jo-Lee Sears, Colleen, Lee Barta, Beth Alfred, Tiffany, Cindy Harcar, Judy Stephens, Susan M. Leedy, Jami Bridgman, Huw, Angie Grafton, Julie Howard, Rachel B, Dannnii Desjarlais, Jeanie, Amanda, Irene Dobson, Annette Estrella, Remy Tankel-Carroll, Jessica Bowman, Sherry Whitaker, Kelley Schroeder, Patricia Jeter, John Arvidsson, Anna, Tim Haight, Joy Page, Donna, Natalie Gwinn, Martyn Heaney, Tara Pendley, Liberty Susan Gabor, Amanda Gallegos, John, Gordon Carmichael, James, Charles Junkin, Nick, Damon Geddins, Toni Marie Rinella, Robin Symes, Merja Mikkonen, Cheryl Posadas, Landa-Lou Goodridge, Wanda Jones, Barbara English, Carol Ryan, Patricia Hallford, Shane Neely, Allyssa Howells, Julanne Neifeld, Jason Barnum, Kurt Brown, Connie White, Muhammad Nizam Bin Mohtar, Cindy Sirois, Teresa, Jason, Amanda, Jannis M. Fetter, Julie Descant, Christopher, Karin Dennis, Lynne Ridley, Sena Schneider, Melissa Swain, Crystaldeloera, Jennifer Hanlon, Shanon Taylor, Dani Bigner, Rita, Pat Eroh, Jennifer Lloyd, Kelly, Amy Steagall Johnson, Brandy Swartz, James T. Cudd, Sai Putnam, Monde Magolo, Anj Panes, Sandra Driskell, Marshall Bellitire, Amanda Kliebert, Ole Pedersen, Joyce Carroll, Dee Simmons, Alexis Osborne, Kristin Schroeder, Jean Black, Michelle Babb, Kim Thurston, Shakila "Kiki" Robinson, Krystal Eldred, Laurel von Dobschutz, Sue Wells, Larry J. Field, Linda Blackburn, Cory Lindsey, Deborah Sparagna, Michelle Lee, Cathy Russell, Sharee Steffens, David Richardson, Sue Wallace, Stefanie Valentine, Tammy Sittlinger, Chris Hurte, Felix Sacco, James Valentine, Shelley Challinor, Mark Sawyer, Thomas Stewart Rae, Kathleen

Tardi, Traci Spelts, Gina L Dorsey, Danny West, Deborah Hanson, Alan Kleynenberg, Tamela L. Matuska, Michael Rilley, Sherry Sundin, Janet A Madison, Stefanie Mathis, Chad Mellor, Monica Bleen, Susan Weaver, Monica Yokel, Linda Shoemaker, Connie Lynn Music, Tina Rattray-Green, Susan Ault, Sharon Fouke, Janine, Samantha Watt, Shelia Clark, Michele Gosselin, Tanya Jack, Karen Smith, Alicia Gir, Judy Morris, Casey Renee Bates, Shannon Fiene, Cara Butcher, Janet Kazimi, Tracy Patterson, Rebecca Roberts, Katelyn Townsend, Jennifer Jones, Lolly Caviness, Leigh Lombardi, Adrian Brown, Marcia Heacock, Lisa Slat, Amy Hart, Richard Allen, Deirdre Green, Tim Hurd, Janet Elam, Paula Lookabill, Bambi Dawn Goggio, Diane Kourajian, Rebecca Mullis, Abriel Miller, Yolanda Benavidez, Jamie Dome, Tammy, Brandy Noble, Jon Wiederhorn, Linda J Evans, Diane Kremski, Tina Bullard, Debbie Cochran, Crystal Clark, Jamie Rasmussen, Rebecca Adams, Myene Kelley, Doreen Marrisett, Melody Sanderson, Awilda Roman, Corey Lea Simpson, Don Price, Patricia Fulton, Eoin Corr, Cindy Selby, Amy Edwards, Debbie Hill, Robyn Byers, Nancy Harrison, Wendy Lippard

Continue Your Exploration Into

The Murderous Minds

Excerpt From List of Twelve Collection 1

I

Marjorie Orbin

"WHAT THIS SEEMS TO BE IS A REVELATION OF your very darkest side, ma'am," said Judge Arthur Anderson, as he stared at Marjorie Orbin during her sentencing hearing. "When that dark side is unleashed, it's about as dark as it gets," he continued.

The judge spoke these words from his bench on September 8th, 2004, in a courtroom in Phoenix, Arizona. It was the start of fall in Arizona, a welcome reprieve from the blistering heat of the summer. It was not only the torrid heat that ended however, but a dark chapter of this desert community's crime annals.

A Grisly Find

The residents of Phoenix enjoy a patchwork of preserved desert areas throughout the city. However, on October 23rd, 2004, the rugged beauty of the area was eclipsed by a morbid find at the corner of Tatum and Dynamite Road, in North Phoenix. The Phoenix Police Department's 911 call center received a panicked call from an individual who was hiking in the area.

Police quickly arrived at the desert location, and the hiker led them to a spot that was not far off from the residential streets that surrounded the reservation. When the officers reached the site, they instantly knew that this was not a routine call. Detective Dave Barnes, of the Missing Persons Unit, arrived on the scene minutes later. A putrid smell filled the air as Barnes walked toward a 50-gallon Rubbermaid bin. "As we walked up you could smell the death in the air. Once you smell it, you know what it is for the rest of your life...it's the first time I had ever seen anything like that, where it's – just a piece of body," he would later say.

Barnes removed the lid and carefully opened the black trash bag contained within. Inside the trash bag was the bloody, dismembered torso of an adult male. Barnes would later tell a reporter, "All of the insides, all of the internal organs, intestines were missing…I thought, 'Who could do this to a human being? Cut off his arms, his legs, his head?'"

The grisly find was located less than two miles from the home of Marjorie Orbin, who lived in the 17000 Block of North 55th Street. Butcher had a strong suspicion that he had just found the torso of her missing husband; Marjorie had filed a missing person's report on September 22nd, 2004.

Jay Orbin was the successful owner of Jayhawk International, a dealership that specialized in Native American Art. He frequently traveled for business purposes, and it was not unusual for him to be gone three weeks out of the month. It was through his business travels that Jay met Marjorie.

The Stripper And The Salesman

Marjorie had been married seven times before meeting Jay at the age of 35. Marjorie was unable to conceive children and had lived a life with herself as the central focus. She entered each relationship looking for her Prince Charming, but it never happened.

Michael J. Peter was a very successful businessman who had made millions creating upscale strip clubs around the world. Marjorie left Peter because she believed he was cheating on her.

She moved to Las Vegas, where she danced at a strip club. It was at this strip club in 1993 that she met Jay, who was traveling through Las Vegas. They had been dating for a while when Jay proposed to Marjorie, offering to pay for fertility treatments if she married him. Marjorie accepted Jay's proposal, and they got married at the Little White Wedding Chapel in Las Vegas.

Soon afterward, they moved to Phoenix, where Jay lived. Marjorie was able to conceive and gave birth to their son, Noah. The couple divorced in 1997 but continued to live together. Marjorie had problems with the IRS and did not want Jay's assets to be vulnerable.

Jay's Disappearance

September 8th, 2004, Jay was driving back to Phoenix from a business meeting when he got a call from his mother, wishing him a happy birthday. That call was the last time anyone spoke to Jay.

When Jay's parents, brothers, and friends called his home, Marjorie told them that he had gone on a business trip and would not be returning until September 20th. During that time, those who cared about Jay could not reach him on his cell phone. His parents and friends expressed their concern to Marjorie; however, she said she did not know what was going on with him.

People who spoke to Marjorie about Jay stated that she expressed little concern for his welfare. Jay's intended return date passed, and still, nobody could reach him. When they inquired with Marjorie, she continued to remain aloof to their concerns. After continued pressure from friends and family, a missing person's report was filed on September 22nd.

Suspicion Is Raised

The Police Department assigned Detective Jan Butcher to the case. She interviewed Marjorie, who indicated that the last time she'd seen Jay was on August 28th, when he had attended his son's birthday. Butcher became suspicious of Marjorie on September 28th, after leaving voicemail messages for her before she called back. "I asked her to provide me the license plate of the vehicle Jay was driving. She said she would call me back. She never did. So, that was a little bit odd," she later told a reporter.

From that point on, Butcher's suspicions only continued to grow. Credit card and phone tower records indicated that Jay had arrived at his home in Phoenix on September 28th, which didn't match Marjorie's claim that she had last seen him on August 28th.

When detectives checked Jay's credit card records, they found that Marjorie was spending thousands of dollars, including purchasing a $12,000 baby grand piano, while the business account had a withdrawal of $45,000. Within one day of reporting Jay missing, she had liquidated a total of $100,000 from Jay's personal and business accounts.

A final cause for suspicion arose during a call that Detective Butcher made to Marjorie requesting that she take a polygraph test. Butcher heard Marjorie remark to someone in the background, "You know what? She wants me to take a polygraph tomorrow." A male voice replied, "You tell her to go f--- herself."

Butcher obtained a search warrant and went to Marjorie's home, accompanied by a SWAT team. The SWAT team forced their way in and encountered an adult male, Larry Weisberg. Larry was Marjorie's new boyfriend and the voice that had been heard in the background of the phone call. Weisberg was combative, resulting in police tasing him.

Police searched the premises and found a large number of credit cards belonging to Jay, plus his business checkbook, items that he always kept with him when traveling. Though police did not make any arrests, their surveillance of Marjorie deepened. It was shortly after Marjorie's home was searched that police found Jay's torso in the Rubbermaid bin in the desert.

DNA evidence confirmed the torso belonged to Jay Orbin. The Maricopa County Medical Examiner's Office inspected the torso and concluded Jay had been shot and his body frozen. At some point, the body had been defrosted, and a jigsaw was used to dismember and decapitate it.

When searching Jay's business, police found a packet of jigsaw blades, with some of the blades missing. The Medical Examiner's Office determined the blades from the business matched the cut marks on the torso, where the limbs and vertebrae were severed.

Detectives traced the UPC code on the Rubbermaid bin back to a Lowes Home Improvement store in Scottsdale. The detectives scored big when they viewed video from the store's surveillance cameras and saw Marjorie purchasing the Rubbermaid bin, trash bags, and black tape. Police detained Marjorie when they caught her forging Jay's signature while making a purchase at a Circuit City store.

Jay's remaining body parts were never found, nor the gun that was used to shoot Jay.

Marjorie and her boyfriend, Larry Weisberg, were arrested on December 6, 2004. Weisberg was offered immunity if he agreed to testify against Marjorie, who was sentenced to life in prison on October 1st, 2009.

 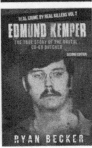 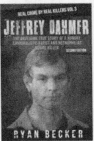 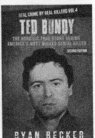

168

About True Crime Seven

True Crime Seven Books is about exploring the stories behind all the murderous minds in the world. From unknown murderers to infamous serial killers. It is our goal to create content that satisfies true crime enthusiasts' morbid curiosities while sparking new ones.

Our writers come from all walks of life but with one thing in common, and that is they are all true crime enthusiasts. You can learn more about them below:

Ryan Becker is a True Crime author who started his writing journey in late 2016. Like most of you, he loves to explore the process of how individuals turn their darkest fantasies into a reality. Ryan has always had a passion for storytelling. So, writing is the best output for him to combine his fascination with psychology and true crime. It is Ryan's goal for his readers to experience the full immersion with the dark reality of the world, just like how he used to in his younger days.

Nancy Alyssa Veysey is a writer and author of true crime books, including the bestselling, *Mary Flora Bell: The Horrific True Story Behind an Innocent Girl Serial Killer*. Her medical degree and work in the field of forensic psychology, along with postgraduate studies in criminal justice, criminology, and pre-law, allow her to bring a unique perspective to her writing.

Kurtis-Giles Veysey is a young writer who began his writing career in the fantasy genre. In late 2018, he parlayed his love and knowledge of history into writing nonfiction accounts of true crime stories that occurred in centuries past. Told from a historical perspective, Kurtis-Giles brings these victims and their killers back to life with vivid descriptions of these heinous crimes.

Kelly Gaines is a writer from Philadelphia. Her passion for storytelling began in childhood and carried into her college career. She received a B.A. in English from Saint Joseph's University in 2016, with a concentration in Writing Studies. Now part of the real world, Kelly enjoys comic books, history documentaries, and a good scary story. In her true-crime work, Kelly focuses on the motivations of the killers and backgrounds of the victims to draw a complete picture of each individual. She deeply enjoys writing for True Crime Seven and looks forward to bringing more spine-tingling tales to readers.

James Parker, the pen-name of a young writer from New Jersey, who started his writing journey with play-writing. He has always been fascinated with the psychology of murderers and how the media might play a role in their creation. James loves to constantly test out new styles and ideas in his writing so one day he can find something cool and unique to himself.

Brenda Brown is a writer and an illustrator-cartoonist. Her art can be found in books distributed both nationally and internationally. She has also written many books related to her graduate degree in psychology and her minor in history. Like many true crime enthusiasts, she loves exploring the minds of those who see the world as a playground for expressing the darker side of themselves—the side that people usually locked up and hid from scrutiny.

Genoveva Ortiz is a Los Angeles-based writer who began her career writing scary stories while still in college. After receiving a B.A. in English in 2018, she shifted her focus to nonfiction and the real-life horrors of crime and unsolved mysteries. Together with True Crime Seven, she is excited to further explore the world of true crime through a social justice perspective.

You can learn more about us and our writers at:

truecrimeseven.com/about

For updates about new releases, as well as exclusive promotions, join True Crime Seven readers' group and you can also **receive a free book today.** Thank you and see you soon.

Sign up at: **freebook.truecrimeseven.com/**

Or **scan QR Code using your phone's camera app.**

Dark Fantasies Turned Reality

Prepare yourself, we're not going to **hold back on details or cut out any of the gruesome truths...**

Made in the USA
Monee, IL
06 November 2024

69535273R00095